FLORENCE NIGHTINGALE
IN EGYPT AND GREECE

"The Pyramids of El-Geezeh from the Southwest," Francis Frith c. 1857 (Scottish National Portrait Gallery)

FLORENCE NIGHTINGALE
IN EGYPT AND GREECE

Her Diary and "Visions"

Michael D. Calabria

State University of New York Press

SUNY Series in Western Esoteric Traditions
David Appelbaum, editor

Cover: *Rest on the Flight into Egypt* (detail), 1879 (18.652), by Luc Olivier Merson, French (1846–1920), oil on canvas (71.8 × 128.4 CM). Bequest of George Golding Kennedy. Courtesy of Museum of Fine Arts, Boston

Published by
State University of New York Press, Albany

For information, address State University of New York Press,
State University Plaza, Albany, NY 12246

Production by Dana Foote
Marketing by Nancy Farrell

Library of Congress Cataloging-in-Publication Data

Nightingale, Florence, 1820–1910.
    Florence Nightingale in Egypt and Greece : her diary and "visions" /
Michael D. Calabria.
        p.   cm. — (SUNY series in Western esoteric traditions)
    Includes bibliographical references (p.   ) and indexes.
    ISBN 0–7914–3115–0 (alk. paper). — ISBN 0–7914–3116–9 (pbk. : alk.
paper)
        1. Nightingale, Florence, 1820–1910—Diaries. 2. Nightingale, Florence,
1820–1910—Religion. 3. Nightingale, Florence, 1820–1910—Psychology.
4. Visions. I. Calabria, Michael D. II. Title. III. Series.
RT37.N5A3   1997
610.73'092—dc20
[B]   96–6296
                                                                      CIP

Have pity on me, have pity on me,
  O you my friends,
for the hand of God has touched me!
                    — Job 19:21

Contents

Illustrations

Acknowledgments

This research was supported in part by a grant from the City University of New York PSC–CUNY Research Award Program. Copyright of Florence Nightingale's papers in the British Library is maintained by the Trustees of the Henry Bonham-Carter Will Trust. I would like to acknowledge the Trust for granting permission to publish this material, and their solicitors, Radcliffes & Co., for their assistance.

A number of individuals have been particularly helpful to me in the course of this project, including Alex Attewell, Curator of the Florence Nightingale Museum, who has provided invaluable assistance and support over the years; Richard Aspin, Curator of Western Manuscripts, Wellcome Institute of the History of Medicine, for his assistance with the Claydon correspondence; and Janet Macrae, New York University School of Nursing, who read the manuscript several times and made helpful suggestions and observations.

I would like to thank the following institutions for their assistance and permission to reproduce photographic and illustrative material: Miriam and Ira D. Wallach Division of Arts, Prints and Photographs, New York Public Library; National Portrait Gallery (London); Scotish National Portrait Gallery; the City of Birmingham Museum and Art Gallery; University of Chicago Press, and Harrasowitz Verlag.

INTRODUCTION

When Florence Nightingale (1820–1910) (fig. 1) led a team of nurses
to the war-torn Crimea in 1854, she revolutionized the field of
nursing and forever transformed military and public health care in
Europe. A brilliant organizer, she created order amid the chaos of
the ill-equipped army hospital at Scutari and introduced sweeping
sanitary reforms, thereby reducing the mortality rate from 42 to 2
percent. Ever aware of the necessity of healing the mind as well as
the body, she established schools and libraries for the soldiers. She
was praised in song and verse, and dubbed 'the Lady with the lamp'
by Longfellow who likened her to Santa Filomena, the 'daughter
of light.' Hailed as a national heroine, she was the first woman to
be awarded the British National Order of Merit (1907). The nursing school she established at St. Thomas's Hospital in London
(1860) became the model for institutions in Europe and the United
States, and her *Notes on Nursing* (1860) has remained a primary
text for nurses. Although best known for her work in the various
aspects of nursing (including training, administration, and hospital design), Nightingale also addressed important social issues, such
as the causes and prevention of prostitution, poverty, and crime
in England as well as effective means of sanitation, irrigation, and
education in India.[1]
    Nightingale's successes came only after she had experi-
enced tremendous psychological and spiritual anguish. For many
years prior to her mission in the Crimea, she struggled to find
meaning in her life and desperately sought a way to manifest her
notion of God's will. She had been born into an upper-class family that divided its time between two estates, spending three
months of the year at Lea Hurst in Derbyshire (fig. 2), six months
at Embley Park in Hampshire (fig. 3), and three months in London for the social season. She received an exemplary education
from her father, a graduate of Cambridge, who instructed her in
German, French, Italian, Latin, and classical Greek, as well as

---

1. W. J. Bishop and Sue Goldie, *A Bio-Bibliography of Florence Nightingale* (London: Dawsons of Pall Mall, 1962).

in history, philosophy, and rudimentary science. Ubiquitous
houseguests, however, generally ten to fifteen at a time when
the family resided at Embley, demanded her presence in the drawing room. While still an adolescent, she tired of this privileged
and purposeless life, and at age 16 she wrote in a private note
that God had called her into His service.[2] Instinctively she knew
that service to God meant service to humanity, but the precise
means of doing so eluded her. She sought advice from a friend,
Christian von Bunsen, an Egyptologist and the Prussian ambassador to the British court (see later), asking him: "What can an
individual do, towards lifting the load of suffering from the helpless and the miserable?"[3]

In response, Bunsen gave her the yearbook of the Institution
of Deaconesses in Kaiserswerth, Germany, a hospital and orphanage served by Protestant sisters (see later). Bunsen had gone
to Kaiserswerth himself in 1844 to find qualified nurses for the
German hospital he had established in London. The thought of
caring for the sick greatly appealed to Florence's desire to perform service, but 'terrified' her mother. In the early nineteenth
century, nurses were little more than servants, often women without family notorious for sexual improprieties and their love of al-
cohol. Such a view is exemplified in the characterization of Sairey
Gamp in Dickens's *Martin Chuzzlewit* (1843) and Grace Poole
in Brontë's *Jane Eyre* (1847), who had "a fault common to a deal
of them nurses and matrons — *she kept a private bottle of gin by
her,* and now and then took a drop over-much." Mrs. Nightingale
thus flatly denied her daughter's request to spend a few months
training as a nurse at the Salisbury Hospital near Embley. Little
did Mrs. Nightingale know that her restless daughter would in
time change this image of nurses. Pensive, withdrawn, and frustrated by the lack of purpose in her life, Florence's behavior became disruptive to the socially prominent Nightingale family.
The impact on a young person of what was perceived to be a divine call must have been extraordinary indeed. Even the most
sympathetic authors have compared mystical experiences to psy-

2. Joann G. Widerquist, "Florence Nightingale's Calling," *Second Opinion* vol. 17,
no. 3 (January 1992): 108–21.
3. Frances Baroness Bunsen, *Memoirs of Baron Bunsen,* (2nd ed. Philadelphia:
J. B. Lippincott, 1869), vol. 2, p. 13.

chopathological disorders.[4] Nightingale's only solace was nursing sick relatives, to whom she fled whenever possible, and attending the sick villagers near her home. By her mid-twenties, her despondency had reached a crisis level, and Florence pathetically petitioned God to end her life:

> Lord thou knowest the creature which thou hast made. Thou knowest that I cannot live—forgive me, God & let me die—this day let me die. It is not for myself that I say this. Thou knowest that I am more afraid to die than to live . . . but I know that by living I shall only heap anxieties on other hearts, which will increase with time.[5]

Even as her agony continued, she began to sense that perhaps there was some purpose to her life:

> God has something for me to do for him—or he would have let me die some time ago. I hope to do it by living—then my eyes would indeed have seen his salvation—but now I am dust & nothing, worse than nothing—a curse to my self & others.[6]

It is important to note that Nightingale's frustrations are not simply those of a repressed Victorian woman but are rather those of a woman who felt called to service by God. To deny her some regular occupation or meaningful activity was to send one of God's missionaries to the stake. In a letter to her cousin Hilary Bonham Carter, she wrote of her frustration and confusion:

> The Kingdom of God is come, I know, Jesus Christ says so, and we feel it—but my life is so full of anxieties, of eager fears about these things which are inextricable, things about which I really don't know *which* I wish,

---

4. Edward Mitchell Podvoll, "Psychosis and the Mystic Path," *The Psychoanalytic Review*, vol. 66, no. 4 (1979): 571–90; Dereck M. Daschke, "Individuation and the Psychology of the Mystic Union," *Journal of Psychology and Christianity*, vol. 12, no. 3 (1993): 245–52.

5. Private note, November 1845 (BM Add. MSS 43402:34).
6. BM Add. MSS 43402:35.

that I kneel down when the sun rises in the morning,
& only say, Behold the handmaiden of the Lord, give
me this day any work, no not my work, but thine to do.
I ask no other blessing. For the things which I ask for I
do not wish & the things I do wish, I know I shan't
have.[7]

Family friends Charles and Selina Bracebridge provided Florence with a temporary respite from her untenable domestic life
with an invitation to travel to Rome in October 1847. While in
Rome, she went on a ten-day retreat at the Convent Trinita de
Monti where she met the Madre Santa Columba, a woman who
would have a lasting effect on her. In spite of her Anglican up-
bringing, Nightingale was drawn to Catholic orders as they provided women in particular with more opportunity for religious service than did the Anglican Church at this time (Anglican sisterhoods
had only recently appeared).[8] She must have sensed her family's
alarm at her interest in Catholicism, and thus wrote defensively:

Are you afraid that I am becoming a Roman Catholic?
I might perhaps, if there had been anything in me for a
Roman Catholic to lay hold of, but I was not a Protestant before . . . Can either of these two [churches] be
true? Can the "word" be pinned down to either one period or one church? All churches are, of course, only
more or less unsuccessful attempts to represent the unseen to the mind.[9]

Despite her protests, four years after this letter was written she
corresponded at length with Henry Manning, whom she had first

---

7. Letter of August 14, 1846 (BM Add. MSS. 45794.f.110). The same sentiment
is repeated in a letter to her aunt Hannah Nicholson (BM Add. MSS 45,794.f.39).
8. Since the English reformation and the dissolution of religious communities
by Henry VIII, the Anglican Church had lacked religious orders. As a result of the
Anglo-Catholic ('Oxford') Movement promulgated by John Henry Newman, there
was renewed interest in Anglican orders in the mid-nineteenth cenutury. C.f.
A. M. Allchin, *The Silent Rebellion: Anglican Religious Communities, 1845–1900*
(London: SCM, 1958).
9. Mary Keele, ed. *Florence Nightingale in Rome: Letters Written by Florence
Nightingale in Rome in the Winter of 1847–1848.* Memoirs of the American Philosophical Society, 143. (Philadelphia: American Philosophical Society, 1981), p. 155.

met in Rome and who had since converted to Catholicism, as she had in mind to do likewise (see conclusion). Twenty years after her trip she would write: "I have never enjoyed any time in my life as much as my time at Rome."[10]

Nightingale's frustrations continued, however, upon her return home in 1848, and thus she welcomed a second invitation from the Bracebridges to travel to Egypt and Greece in the winter of 1849.[11] Often blaming herself for the domestic squabbles, she viewed her journey to Egypt as an opportunity to establish some order in her life and thereby restore peace to the family. On the eve of her departure she wrote to her mother from Marseilles: "I hope I shall come back to be more a comfort to you than ever I have been."[12] Even though removed from the scene of domestic conflict, during her trip she experienced much inner torment as she wrestled with her divine calling. She recorded her activities and her thoughts for this period in a diary that she began in Egypt in January 1850 and concluded in August of that year upon her return home. As is evident from the diary, this was a cathartic and critical period for her: in Egypt, God 'spoke' to her on several occasions, and she meditated earnestly on the words of her 'madre' Santa Columba whom she had met in Rome; in Greece, she met another woman who had a profound influence on her, the American missionary Mrs. Hill; and, on the return journey through Germany, she made her first visit to the Institution of Deaconesses at Kaiserswerth, an experience that firmly set her feet upon the road to nursing.

---

10. Letter to Mme. Mohl, November 21, 1869 (Sir Edward Cook, *The Life of Florence Nightingale* (London: Macmillan, 1913), vol. 1, p. 79.

11. Florence's relationship with the Bracebridges remained close to the end of their lives. They accompanied her to the Crimea in 1854. Charles died in 1872 and Selina in 1874. Florence wrote of them: "He and she have been the creators of my life. . . . And when I think of Atherstone [the Bracebridge home], of Athens, of all the places I have been in with them, of the immense influence they had in shaping my own life—more than earthly mother and father to me—I cannot doubt that they leave behind them, having shaped many lives as they did mine, their mark on the century. . . ." (Sir Edward Cook, *The Life of Florence Nightingale*, vol. 2, p. 236).

12. Letter to Mrs. Nightingale, November 1849 (from a copy at the Wellcome Institute for the History of Medicine, London).

For a discussion of the effects of Eastern travel, see Maria H. Frawley's "Desert Places/Gendered Spaces: Victorian Women in the Middle East," *Nineteenth Century Contexts*, vol. 15, no. 1 (1991): 49–64; and Joan Rees's *Writings on the Nile: Harriet Martineau, Florence Nightingale, Amelia Edwards* (London: Rubicon, 1995).

Whereas the significance of this diary has been noted, only a few excerpts have hitherto been published.[13] Although the most interesting (and longest) diary entries are those in which Nightingale describes her spiritual struggles, they present only part of the picture. In its complete form, the diary allows us to see her struggles as they erupted in the midst of her everyday activities. On several occasions she was on the verge of physical and mental collapse and driven to the very brink of sanity. I have thus opted to include the whole contents of the diary here, accompanied by a detailed analysis and supplemented by unpublished letters and notes, as it places her experiences in a larger (and more accurate) context as has not been done before. The diary contains a record of the places she visited; of mundane activities, such as letter writing or reading; as well as an intimate account of her psycho-spiritual battles.

The contrast between the earlier and later entries is stark. Whereas the entries for January and much of February contain brief lists or simple descriptions of the sights and people encountered along the way with only fleeting references to her spiritual crisis, the entries for March and early April become increasingly contemplative. After a circuitous voyage from Egypt to Greece via Italy, her crisis continued and came to a climax in May and June. In July her spirits improved as she was occupied with visits to hospitals in Berlin and Hamburg, and then finally Kaiserswerth.

Whereas her diary served as a personal record of her trip, she presented an 'official' version of her travels to her family in copious letters. Indeed the difference in tone between the diary and the letters to her family led Nancy Boyd to remark in her study of Nightingale: "When one correlates the entries in the diary with the dates of the letters, one realizes the degree to which the inner

---

13. Joann Widerquist noted that Nightingale's writings, "especially from Egypt, indicated the intense struggles she was undergoing" ("The Spirituality of Florence Nightingale," *Nursing Research*, vol. 41, no. 1, January/February 1992). Although Sir Edwin Cook's two-volume biography of Nightingale (1913) in many ways remains the most comprehensive study of her life and work, he speaks only briefly of her trip to Egypt and the diary. Various excerpts of the diary can be found in: I. B. O'Malley's *Florence Nightingale: 1820–1856* (1931); Cecil Woodham-Smith's *Florence Nightingale: 1829–1910* (1951), with errors and ommisions; and more recently in *Ever Yours, Florence Nightingale: Selected Letters* (Martha Vicinus and Bea Nergaard, eds., 1990), and in Joann Widerquist's "Florence Nightingale's Calling" (*Second Opinion*, vol. 17, no. 3 [January 1992]: 108–21).

self that tormented her was kept hidden behind the outward self she displayed to her parents."[14]

More than simply being eloquent descriptions of her journey, however, the letters are remarkable for their erudite discussions of ancient Egyptian and Greek religion and philosophy, as well as Christianity, and clearly demonstrate that Nightingale was preoccupied with theological and philosophical issues during her voyage. These expositions were not merely intellectual exercises; by means of these discourses, she honed and refined her own spiritual philosophy. It is during this time that she began writing a draft of a work that explored the nature of God and humanity's relationship to God. Printed in 1852, this sixty-five-page proof merely served as the core of what was to become a vast religious-philosophical treatise comprising three volumes and totaling over 800 pages. Titled *Suggestions for Thought to the Searchers After Truth Among the Artizans of England*, it was to be the most complete explication of her spirituality, an eclectic mix of Platonism, Christian mysticism, Positivism, and Rationalism.[15]

In 1987 Anthony Sattin produced an edited version of Nightingale's letters from Egypt, admitting that he had excluded "the longer passages where she discusses philosophical and theosophical issues."[16] In some cases the passages excluded from Sattin's edition are suggestive of the very struggle is evident from her diary entries and introduce concepts discussed at length in *Suggestions for Thought*. Although she by no means revealed her spiritual callings and conflicts to her family in the letters, she did nevertheless raise issues that concerned or troubled her. By correlating the diary entries with some unpublished passages from her letters, we may be able to reconstruct the intellectual, psychological, and spiritual state in which Nightingale realized her ambitions.

Sattin also excluded from his edition a piece of fiction titled *Vision of Temples*, which Nightingale had written in Egypt and which was appended to the 1854 edition of her letters (that her

14. *Three Victorian Women Who Changed Their World: Josephine Butler, Octavia Hill, Florence Nightingale* (New York: Oxford university Press, 1982), p. 176.

15. *Suggestions for Thought: Selections and Commentaries*, edited by Michael D. Calabria and Janet A. Macrae (Philadelphia: University of Pennsylvania Press, 1994).

16. *Letters from Egypt: a Journey on the Nile, 1849–1850* (New York: Weidenfeld & Nicolson, 1987), p. 9.

sister Parthenope had printed and distributed much to Florence's dismay). At first glance, the *Vision* appears to be little more than an imaginative tale of ancient Egypt wrought by an enthusiastic tourist. Sattin failed to recognize, however, that this fantasy merely serves as a vehicle by which Nightingale conveys the metaphysical essence of her own radical spiritual views. The text of *Vision of Temples* and discussion comprise Part II of this volume. Finally, Part III comprises a brief work that Nightingale composed while in Greece and that I have titled "A Greek Vision." It is noteworthy for her eloquent answer to that question of the ages: "What is the meaning of Life?"

As will be seen, remarks in her diary, letters from Egypt, *Vision of Temples*, "Greek vision," and *Suggestions for Thought* indicate that Nightingale was essentially a mystic. At the heart of her spiritual creed was a belief in an omnipotent spirit of righteousness (God) whose very thoughts were manifest as immutable laws. By means of these laws, humanity rises from the imperfect to the perfect and thus becomes an incarnation of the Divine: "In accordance with God's law, human consciousness is tending to become what God's consciousness is — to become one with the consciousness of God."[17] Taken as a whole, her philosophical and spiritual interests are also highly indicative of her mysticism: while still in her teens she translated Plato's works, and many years later provided renowned classical scholar Benjamin Jowett with considerable assistance in his own translations of the *Dialogues;* of the Scriptures, the Gospel of John (considered to be the most mystical of the Gospels) impressed her the most; she was interested in Hermetism and Gnosticism of the late pagan and early Christian period (see discussion in the commentary); and she read and translated the works of various medieval mystics, whose writings she later intended to comprise an anthology to be titled *Notes from Devotional Authors of the Middle Ages* (see later).

In her classic study of mysticism, Evelyn Underhill identified five phases in the mystical life, some of which are applicable to Nightingale's spiritual development: (1) awakening, (2) purgation, (3) illumination, (4) the 'Dark Night of the Soul,' and

---

17. *Suggestions for Thought* (Calabria & Macrae, eds.), p. 58. For discussion, see pp. xii–xv.

(5) union.[18] The transition from one stage to the next is generally a gradual unfolding and thus the phases may overlap. 'Awakening' denotes the initial mystical conversion in which one undergoes a dramatic shift in consciousness, signaling the surrender of one's personal will to that of God. Commonly this occurs after a period of restlessness or dissatisfaction such as that experienced by Nightingale in her youth. Often this change in consciousness is accompanied by visions or auditions, such as the blinding light and voices experienced by Paul of Tarsus at his conversion (Acts 9:1–9) or the crucifix of San Damiano, which called to Francis of Assisi. Nightingale's 'awakening' clearly commences with the first call from God she experienced at age sixteen.

In the purgative stage, the individual, having awakened to a sense of the Divine, realizes her imperfection and separation from the One and seeks to rid herself of all egoistic attachments and desires. "It is in this torment of contrition," Underhill wrote, ". . . that we have the first swing back from the initial state of mystic pleasure to the complimentary state of pain."[19] In May 1850 particularly, Nightingale experienced both psychological pain *and* physical weakness. Consumed with her failings, she, like many mystics before her, entreated God with vows of chastity and obedience (May 12).

The pain of Purgation gives way to Illumination, characterized by increased feelings of peace and joy. In these instances the individual undergoes a change in consciousness from being self-centered to God-centered. As Underhill indicates, however, Purgation and Illumination often co-exist in the individual experience, states of depression alternating with delight.[20] We shall see Nightingale in utter despair on June 18 cry out that "all is in vain," and then two days later write "I lived again. . . . I was free." This stage is also characterized by a spiritual 'betrothal' in which the soul contemplates union with the Absolute. We will see the intimate language that Nightingale used to describe her relationship with God. Thus, according to Underhill's model and based upon the diary entries, we witness Nightingale in the midst of 'purgation' and 'illumination.'

---

18. *Mysticism* (New York: New American Library, 1974), pp. 169 ff.
19. Ibid., p. 201.
20. Ibid., p. 227.

Oscillating between states of great pain and intense joy, it is during the 'illuminative' stage that the mystic commonly hears voices or engages in dialogues with God, such as those Nightingale experienced beginning in February. Teresa of Avila, with whose writings Nightingale was quite familiar, cautioned her readers against locutions that originated in the intellect or from melacholia rather than coming from God.[21] She indicated that genuine auditions "dispose the soul and prepare it from the very beginning, and they touch it, give it light, favor it and bring it quiet"; genuine words from God are listened to rather than composed, they effect what they say ("those the Lord speaks are both words and works"), and such locutions are fixed in the memory for a very long time, if not permanently. Nightingale remembered vividly the occasions on which God called to her, recalling them in 1867 and again in 1892 — fifty-five years after God first spoke to her.[22]

Despite her own communications from God, and her great love and admiration of medieval mysticism, Nightingale, ever of a practical mind, was skeptical of 'ecstatic states.' Many years later, in her *Notes from Devotional Authors of the Middle Ages*, she would write:

> It is very plain how 'ecstacies' were bred in people half-starved by long fastings & long watchings. So far from wondering that these half-starved people believed in their Visions, we wonder that they had not more.
> The 'mystical' state — by which we understand the drawing near to God by means of — not Church or Ceremony but — the state in which we keep, through God's Laws, our own soul — is real & should be permanent.
> The 'ecstatic' state is unreal, & should not be at all.[23]

Some studies of Nightingale would reduce her mystical experiences to a psychopathology, to hysteria, "peculiar to the Victorian bourgeois woman, wherein rage is passively turned inward

21. *Book of Her Life* (ch. 25) and *The Interior Castle* (part 6, chapter 3).
22. Widerquist, "Florence Nightingale's Calling," p. 110.
23. BM Add. MSS 45841.f.17.

and expressed through the body."[24] There is no question that Nightingale experienced much pain and frustration from the boundaries imposed upon her by her family and by a repressive society that gave women few opportunities—this much she tells us herself, most vividly in "Cassandra," in volume two of her *Suggestions for Thought*.[25] It would be a gross oversimplification, however, to simply attribute Nightingale's mystical experiences to personal frustrations. From an early age, she displayed mystical tendencies in thought and temperment concurrent with her need for meaningful activity—tendencies that remained with her throughout her life, long after she had freed herself from the confines of her family and was active in military health-care reform. To reduce Nightingale's auditions to nothing more than a symptom of hysteria, we would be forced to likewise regard the passionate and stirring accounts of voices and visions as related by Teresa of Avila, Angela of Foligno, Catherine of Siena, Gertrud of Helfta, and the scores of other women throughout the world who claim to have experienced transcendence. While he himself was not entirely convinced by mystical states, psychologist and philosopher William James was compelled to admit at the turn of the century: "the existence of mystical states absolutely overthrows the pretension of non-mystical states to be the sole and ultimate dictators of what we may believe."[26]

---

24. Jennifer Shaddock, 'Florence Nightingale's *Notes on Nursing* as Survival Memoir," *Literature and Medicine*, vol. 14, no. 1 (Spring 1995): 23–35. See also Elaine Showalter, *The Female Malady: Women, Madness, and English Culture, 1830–1980* (New York: Penguin, 1985).

25. Published also as an appendix to Ray Strachey's *The Cause* (1928) and by the Feminist Press in 1979. See also Mary Poovey's *Cassandra and Other Selections from Suggestions for Thought* (1992).

26. *The Varieties of Religious Experience* (New York: Collier, 1961), p. 335.

PART I

The Diary

Although Europeans had been traveling to Egypt for centuries seeking treasure and adventure or as part of a pilgrimage to the Holy Land, travel was often dangerous. When the Scotsman James Bruce arrived in Egypt in 1768 to search for the source of the Nile, he was compelled to dress *à la turc* in order to avoid detection and harassment by *banditti,* and walled monasteries provided the safest accommodations. Egypt changed dramatically, however, following Napoleon's invasion in 1798 and the subsequent British occupation as the country was drawn into the arena of European politics. As the American tourist John Lloyd Stephens observed: "Here the long-cherished animosity of France and England sought a new battle-field, as if conscious that the soil of Europe had too often been moistened with human blood."[1]

Having destroyed the power of the Ottoman Mamluk sultans, Napoleon introduced sweeping reforms in the administration of Egypt by inviting the participation of local Egyptian leaders; roads and factories were built, public health and sanitation improved, and a national Arabic press was created. The defeat of the French by the British at Aboukir in 1801 provided Muhammad Ali with the opportunity to consolidate his own position in Egypt, becoming the Ottoman Viceroy in 1805. His economic and military reforms based on European models created a stable land that grew increasingly attractive to western tourists. Upon meeting the Pasha in 1835, John Lloyd Stephens remarked that:

> everybody had great curiosity to visit that interesting country; that heretofore it had been very difficult to get there, and dangerous to travel in when there; but now the facilities of access were greatly increased, and traveling in Egypt had become so safe under his government, that strangers would soon come with as much confidence as they felt while traveling in Europe.[2]

1. John Lloyd Stephens, *Incidents of Travel in Egypt, Arabia Petraea, and the Holy Land,* edited with an introduction by Victor Wolfgang von Hagen (San Francisco: Chronicle Books, 1991), p. 9.
2. Ibid., p. 20.

Eager to sustain and improve their commercial and military access to India via Egypt, the British established transit agencies to assist people traveling between Alexandria, Cairo, and Suez. By the 1840s European and American travelers to Egypt numbered in the thousands.[3]

When Napoleon invaded Egypt, French *savants* scoured the country drawing, copying, and measuring the ancient monuments. Their findings, published as *Description de L'Égypte* (1809–13) inspired British and German Egyptologists to follow suit. John Gardner Wilkinson (1797–1875) made numerous expeditions to Egypt between 1821 and 1842 copying inscriptions and paintings from tombs and other monuments. He authored several major books on Egyptology, including *Topography of Thebes and General View of Egypt* (1835), *Manners and Customs of the Ancient Egyptians* (3 vols., 1837), and his popular guidebook *Modern Egypt and Thebes*, which Nightingale read during her voyage up the Nile.

German Egyptologist Karl Richard Lepsius (1810–84) led an historic expedition to Egypt in 1843–45 under the tutelage of Kaiser Wilhelm IV, the findings of which were published in twelve monumental volumes titled *Denkmäler aus Ägypten und Äthiopien* (1849–59). Nightingale consulted other works by Lepsius, such as his *Chronologie der Ägypter* (1849). Additionally, she read works by her friend (and Lepsius's teacher) Christian von Bunsen (1791–1860) (fig. 4), particularly his *Egypt's Place in Universal History* (5 vols., 1848–60). In addition to being an Egyptologist and Orientalist, Bunsen served as the Prussian ambassador to the Court of St. James from 1842 to 1854. His home in London was a center of great scholarly discourse, and he proved to be of considerable importance to Nightingale's intellectual and spiritual development. As mentioned earlier, Bunsen encouraged her interest in nursing and provided her with information on the Institution of Deaconesses at Kaiserswerth, which she would visit before returning to England in 1850. Through her friendship with Bunsen, Nightingale became familiar with the spiritual traditions of the Near and Far East.

In addition to Egyptological works, during her voyage on the Nile, Nightingale also read a travel account written by Harriet Martineau (1802–76) titled *Eastern Life: Past and Present*, pub-

---

3. The Suez Canal was not completed until 1869. Anthony Sattin, *Lifting the Veil: British Society in Egypt, 1768–1956*, (London: J. M. Dent & Sons, 1988), p. 48.

lished in 1848. Martineau, a friend of Nightingale's maternal aunt Julia Smith, was a prolific writer of fiction and travel books, as well as works on history, politics, religion and social issues. In 1846 Martineau traveled to Egypt with friends Mr. and Mrs. Richard Yates. For both Martineau and Nightingale, the journey to Egypt was as much a psychic one as it was physical, providing an opportunity to wrestle with their unconventional religious views. Martineau wrote that "a Nile voyage is as serious a labour as the mind and spirit can be involved in"[4] and often wandered off by herself for reflection as did Nightingale. Both authors entered into lengthy discourses on Egyptian religion, deriving great inspiration from the ancient beliefs and remarking on the present flaws of Christian doctrine. In light of what they learned of ancient Egyptian religion, Martineau and Nightingale were compelled to reevaluate the singularity of Christianity. They would discover many elements of Egyptian theology in Judaism and Christianity, as well as in Greek philosophy. As such, Martineau considered it "necessary to go back to Egypt for the key."[5] *Eastern Life*, like Nightingale's letters from Egypt, is therefore much more than a travelogue. As will be seen in the course of discussion, Martineau's book proved to be of great interest to Nightingale. (Some years later, Martineau would come to admire Nightingale's plans for public health reform and popularized them in the press. Sharing common concerns, the two corresponded on a variety of social issues.)[6]

Nightingale also turned to the writings of Henry Martyn during her travels. Martyn (1781–1812), an Anglican missionary and chaplain of the East India Company, traveled to India and Persia where he translated the New Testament into Hindustani and Persian. Nightingale read his *Memoirs*, (first published in 1819 with many subsequent editions), quoting him in her diary entry of May 13. Martyn and Nightingale expressed similar sentiments in their writings: both possessed deepfelt piety, earnestly struggled to align their wills with that of God through service, and lamented their weaknesses. Both marked the anniversary of

---

4. *Eastern Life: Past and Present* (London: Edward Moxon, 1848), vol. 1, p. 86.
5. Ibid., vol. 3, p. 107.
6. See Sue Goldie, *A Calendar of Letters of Florence Nightingale* (Oxford: Oxford Microform Publications, 1983), and Martha Vicinus and Bea Nergaard (eds.), *Ever Yours, Florence Nightingale: Selected Letters* (Cambridge: Cambridge University Press, 1990).

the date when God called them into his service, and on the occasion of their thirtieth birthdays, both recalled the life of Christ.
Nightingale's remarks of May 12, 1850, are in fact so similar to
those made by Martyn on the occasion of his thirtieth birthday
as to suggest 'unconscious spiritual plagiarism.' He wrote: "This
day I finished the thirtieth year of my unprofitable life. . . . I am
now at the age at which the Saviour of men began his ministry,'"[7]
and she: "To day I am 30 — the age Christ began his mission."

'Laden with learned books,' including works by Wilkinson,
Bunsen, Lepsius, Martineau, and Martyn as well as Charlotte Brontë
and William Cowper (see later), Nightingale and the Bracebridges
landed at Alexandria on November 18, 1849. There, in addition to
the usual sightseeing, she spent a great deal of time with the sisters of St. Vincent de Paul — not for religious reasons but because
of their nursing practice: "they bleed, dress wounds, and dispense
medicines." Yet, she was touched by a children's mass where she
observed "people of all nations and tongues uniting in the worship
of one God."[8] From Alexandria they boarded a steam-tug that carried them via the Mahmoudieh Canal to the Rosetta branch of the
Nile. The travelers then continued on to Cairo where they boarded
their *dahabiah* (christened 'Parthenope' in honor of Florence's sister) and set sail up the Nile. Making only a few brief stops, they
would sail to Egypt's southern frontier, marked by the rock-cut
temples of Rameses II at Abu Simbel, and then slowly make their
way back northward down the Nile, visiting archaeological sites
along the way.

Nightingale's diary begins after the party reached Thebes
where they stayed overnight in order to explore the Temple of
Luxor before continuing southward. Although these early entries
contain rather sketchy accounts of her activities, even the very
first entry subtly indicates that Nightingale was preoccupied with
other matters. This is evident from her reference to 'dreaming,'
which had been a problem for her since her youth and continued
to be so during her trip and thereafter. 'Dreaming' is probably the
'enemy' she refers to (March 21, June 18), and also the 'murderer
of her thoughts' (March 15). Undoubtedly, she was dreaming of

---

7. *Memoir of the Rev. Henry Martyn* (New York: Protestant Episcopal Society
for the promotion of Evangelical Knowledge, 1858), pp. 257–58.
8. *Letters from Egypt*, p. 6 (1854 ed.); p. 24 (Sattin's ed.)

the manner in which she might serve God, that is through nursing, and how she might accomplish it given her family's objections. Later, in her feminist polemic titled "Cassandra," she would write:

> Women dream till they have no longer the strength to dream; those dreams against which they so struggle, so honestly, vigorously, and conscientiously, and so in vain, yet which are their life, without which they could not have lived; those dreams go at last.[9]

The diary itself (BM Add. MSS 45,846) is an 'Agenda-Moniteur ou Carnet de Poche' for 1850 printed in Paris by E. Marc-Aurel. According to a letter to her mother in November 1849, Nightingale purchased the diary in Marseilles before embarking on the voyage to Egypt.[10] On the inside cover, she has written: "F.N.'s Diary 1850. Egypt &c." As the diary is quite small, measuring just 5¼ × 3¼ inches, in several instances she has taken up the space allotted for several days' notes with her thoughts of a single day. The entries for January to the beginning of March are for the most part written in pen and thereafter in pencil. The handwriting is quite small as a result of the diary's size and in a few cases illegible. In the transcription following, illegible words are indicated by dashes enclosed in square brackets [— — —]. Words or phrases that have been added for clarification or that were lacking in the original but required by context are also enclosed in square brackets. Doubtful readings are indicated by a question mark in square brackets [?]. The months and days that were printed in the diary in French are here given in English. Given her proficiency in several languages, Nightingale occasionally resorted to French and German in her diary. Translations of foreign words and expressions appear in square brackets alongside the original, whereas translations of longer sentences have been placed in footnotes. Words abbreviated by Nightingale (eveng for "evening," cd for "could," wd for "would," etc.) have been rendered in full for ease in reading.

---

9. *Suggestions for Thought* (1860 ed.), vol. 2, p. 403.
10. Letter of November 1849 (from a copy in the Wellcome Institute for the History of Medicine, London).

Other than these exceptions and the accompanying commentary, all other text is original to the diary. Nightingale is inconsistent in her transliteration of Egyptian place names (e.g., Aboo Simbel and Ipsamboul, being in fact the same location). These variations are retained here. Individuals named in the diary have been identified whenever possible. On the end sheets of the diary, Nightingale jotted down notes relating to religious matters. As they are disjointed and without context, they are not included here.

"F.N.'S DIARY 1850. EGYPT &C."

January 1850

Thebes
1. Tuesday
6½   Wrote home
8½   Temple Luxor[11]
10   Wrote home; breakfast; stood on poop.
12   Left — read to Σ[12] Wilkinson & Martineau[13] (Carnac)
4   Dined on deck — read Survey of Thebes & sat on deck
6 (¼)   slept
8½   supper
9½   washing & <u>dreaming</u>
10½   bed

2. Wednesday
7   Temple of Armant (Hermonthis)[14]
8½   Breakfast

---

11. The temple of Luxor, dedicated to the god Amun, was built by Amenhotep III (1390–52 B.C.) and Rameses II (1279–12 B.C.). Nightingale and the Bracebridges would spend more time exploring the temple upon their return journey down the Nile in February [see later].

12. Σ indicates Selina, the wife of Charles Bracebridge, whom Nightingale designated by the Greek letter throughout her diary and correspondence.

13. For Wilkinson and Martineau, see introduction above pp. 16–17.

14. The temple of Armant, which received it latest additions under Cleopatra VII (51–30 B.C.), was still standing in the nineteenth century. It has since been destroyed.

9½   Reading Wilkinson to ∑ & Lepsius with Mr. B.[15]
1½   Wrote home
2 (¼) Writing
3   dinner and wrote home till
7   read Arabian Nights to Mr. B. & supper till
10   finished Epicurean till
12   passed Esne with a fair wind
      obliged to stop till moon rose —
      then ran aground — & stuck till morning

3. Thursday
7½   Wrote letters
9   breakfast & making plans for journey
12   [reading] Bunsen with Mr. B.
3   dinner
4   letters (¼) & journal
anchored off Edfoo

4. Friday
Walked before breakfast. [Reading] Bunsen all day. Making
an analysis of the Dynasties. The hottest weather we have
had.

5. Saturday
Hagar Silsilis[16] — saw the little rock corridor before breakfast.
Bunsen's Dynasties all day.

6. Sunday
Asouan 12 noon. I[sland]. of Elephantine. Evening walk in Syene.
Wrote home.

7. Monday
Cataracts 9–½ p[ast] 1. Philae. Wrote home.

8. Tuesday
Began Bunsen again & his hard work. Kalabsheh. Entered the
tropic.

---

15. I.e., Charles Bracebridge.
16. Gebel el-Silsila, site of ancient sandstone quarries.

9. Wednesday
Bunsen all day. Paolo[17] gave me my poor little chameleon—it
slept on my bed.

10. Thursday
Bunsen. First walk in Nubia. Chameleon very miserable—would
not eat.

11. Friday
Bunsen. Chameleon caught his first fly. Korosko—Pacha's tents
there on his way to Darfur.[18]

12. Saturday
Bunsen all day. Calm—towing—exceedingly warm delightful
weather 110° on deck 88° in cabin.

13. Sunday
Bunsen. Walk on shore among the Castor Oils—human[19] &
vegetable. Stopped at Derr—saw the temple in the rock—
Capital of the Laputae.[20]

14. Monday
Finished my History of the XXXI Dyns. of Egypt for Mr.
Bracebridge. Began Lepsius.

---

17. According to a letter of November 14, 1849, Paolo was a Maltese who had
traveled with the Nightingales fifteen years earlier, and "has been up the Nile almost every winter since." See Sue Goldie, *Calendar of the Letters of Florence
Nightingale* (Oxford, 1983), 2.E13,456. He is almost certainly the same Paolo Nuozzo,
the Maltese servant who accompanied American tourist John Lloyd Stephens to
Egypt in 1835. In his popular travel account, Stephens wrote of him: "He was a
man about thirty-five years old . . . a passionate admirer of ruins, particularly the
ruins of the Nile. . . . He had lived several years in Cairo, and had traveled on the
Nile before, and understood all the little arrangements necessary for the voyage"
(*Incidents of Travel in Egypt*, pp. 39–40).

18. The *pacha* (or pasha) refers to Abbas I, grandson of Muhammad Ali. A despot
and generally suspicious of Europeans, he did little to carry on the reforms begun
by his grandfather. He was murdered at the hands of his servants in 1854.

19. Nightingale is referring to the Nubian practice of applying castor oil to the
hair and skin.

20. A rock-cut temple of Rameses II is located at Derr. The 'capital of the Laputae' is a reference to Jonathan Swift's *Gulliver's Travels*. According to the story,

On January 15, the travelers reached the southernmost point of their voyage, Abu Simbel (var., Aboo Simbel, Ipsamboul), where they visited the rock-cut temples of Rameses II (1279–1212 B.C.) and his queen, Nefretari. Nightingale was deeply impressed with the temples, writing that she "felt more *at home*, perhaps, than in any place of worship" she was ever in.[21] Rather than merely describing the temples to her family, she entered into a lengthy theological discourse of good and evil. Believing evil to be a necessary part of the developmental process in the evolution of human consciousness, she explained that "evil is not the opposer of the good, but its *collaborateur*—the left hand of God, as the good is His right."[22]

She then continued with a discussion of man's relationship with God, using a scene from the temple to illustrate her point. The scene she described depicts Rameses:

> entering the presence of a trinity of gods, I think the sublimest ideal of prayer that ever entered the mind of man to conceive—not shrinking, not awe-struck, he is not even kneeling, not supplicating for forgiveness in that mean and selfish spirit which says, 'Hide thy face from my sins,' instead of saying, 'turn all the light of thy countenance upon my sins, that in that light I may see them, and accepting their consequences, take those consequences as the means to correct them; but raising one hand a little, he stands with face upturned and head uncovered, reverentially offering a reasonable service. . . . Would that I could have understood all that that glorious, yet perfectly human, countenance conveyed . . . the

---

Lagado, the metropolis of Laputae, is a city of strangely built houses in disrepair. C.f. letter of January 21, 1850 (*Letters from Egypt*, 1854 ed., p. 158):

> And I have never so much as mentioned his temple at Derr (the capital of Nubia), hewn in the rock, where he [Rameses II] appears with his faithful lion. But I really don't remember it; I only remember looking out between the portico columns, and thinking that I was in the capital of the Laputae, or some other of Gulliver's countries—so strange, so little like the dwellings of human beings did this capital look.

21. Letter of March 1850, *Letters from Egypt*, p. 290.
22. Letter of January 17, 1850, ibid., p. 128.

mind, which does not offer praise, tiresome praise to God, but says, after its great prototype, 'I and my Father are one,' for his will is one with God, whatever may befall. . . . The Rameses is that of a perfect intellectual and spiritual man, who feels his connection with that of God, whose first and last lesson through His Christ has been, 'Be *one with* me,' not be my instrument, nor my worshipper, nor my petitioner, but *one* with me. I am glad to have seen that representation of prayer, it has taught me more than all the sermons I ever read."[23]

Humanity's relationship with God was of primary interest to her, and she later addressed this very subject in her *Suggestions for Thought:*

The word *"worship,"* however, seems hardly to express what God wants of us. He does not want to be praised, to be adored, to have his glory sung. . . . What he desires seems to be accordance with Him, that we should be one with Him, not prostrate before Him. . . . I would try to teach a child — not to "submit" to God, nor to pray that anything should be otherwise — but to second Him. I would try to inspire it with the idea that it, the child, can second GOD![24]

The entries for the first few months of Nightingale's diary are frustratingly brief and contain cryptic references to making some kind of 'vow' and dreaming 'in the very face of God' at Abu Simbel.

15. Tuesday
Came in sight of Aboo Simbel [fig. 7] with a fair wind soon after 9. Made up our minds to go no further. Walked a long way south to take my last look Abyssinia wards — Sacrifice in the Temple.[25]

---

23. Ibid., pp. 138–40. (This passage was not included in Sattin's edition.)
24. *Suggestions for Thought* (Calabria & Macrae), p. 125.
25. The 'sacrifice' is described in the letter of January 17, 1850 to her family:

16. Wednesday
At sunrise, before the Colossi [fig. 8]. Osirides [i.e. the Osiris columns in the temple] lighted up. Made a vow in the sacred place. Dreadful fights with Trout.[26]

17. Thursday
Sunrise in the Osiris hall. Sailed at 9. Wrote letters — Dreamed in the very face of God.

18. Friday
Long morning with Mr. B. making out his notes of Ipsamboul [i.e. Abu Simbel] & plan — Nicholsons came on board. Pleasant evening by myself — they all at Ibreem[27] — such a sunset.

19. Saturday
Wrote about Ipsamboul. Went on shore to see the dromos of sphynxes at Sabora.[28]

20. Sunday
Rowed in the little boat to see the temple of Hermes Trismegistus [fig. 9].[29]
        Letter from home. One of my 3 chameleons died. I had got for the first two companions.[sic]
        Phthah's temple cave at Jerf Hossayn. Oh heavenly fire, purify me — free me from this slavery.

In the evening we made a great fire upon the altar [in the temple at Abu Simbel], and while our turbaned crew fed it, we sat in the entrance on the top of our hillock, and enjoyed the sight and feeling of the ancient worship restored. (Letters from Egypt, 1854 ed., p. 141).

26. Her female servant during the voyage.
27. Qasr Ibrim — a site marked by an ancient fortress, a temple of Taharqa (690–64 B.C.) and rock-cut shrines.
28. Wadi el-Sebu'a, the site of a temple of Amun and Re-Horakhte built by Rameses II.
29. A temple at Dakka dedicated to Thoth, called 'Hermes Trismegistus' by the Greeks (see p.27).

Nightingale's personal distress at this time is clearly indicated by the plea to be freed from 'this slavery,' a reference perhaps to her unrelenting thoughts of fulfilling some kind of purpose in life and escaping the confines of her upper-class lifestyle. The 'temple cave' referred to above is a structure built by Rameses II at Gerf Hossein dedicated to the god Ptah. As Ptah (var., Phthah) was identified by the Greeks with their god Hephaistos, the Vulcan, Nightingale thus described the temple of Ptah as the dwelling of "Heavenly Fire" to which the purified spirit would return:

> In the solemn twilight we entered the awful cave of Phthah, the God of Fire, the Creator. The shekh of the village, with his descendants, walked before us, carrying great serpents of fire to light up the rude magnificence of this great terrible place. The serpents were thick twisted coils of palm fibre set on fire; but they looked like Moses' serpent set up in the wilderness; and twisted and flamed before this fire shrine, this God of the Hidden Fire, who has his dwelling in the thick darkness. . . . I should like to have seen this dwelling of the "Heavenly Fire" (who will some day welcome back the "tired spirit" to its "accustomed home," and refine away all but the pure ore) in silence and stillness, for I can tell you nothing about the temple.[30]

This very letter, alluded to in the next entry, continued with a lengthy exposition on the metaphysical significance of Ptah and Egyptian ideas concerning creation.

21. Monday
Wrote Hermes Trismegistus letter.
In the afternoon to Kalabsheh & Beit el Wellee — a little gem of the great Rameses. Kalabsheh a vulgar extravagance of the Romans. Rapids of Kalabsheh by moonlight — the wildest scene — battle of the crew.[31]

---

30. Letter of January 21, 1850, *Letters from Egypt*, 1854 ed., pp. 148–49.

31. Reference to a brawl that broke out on board during the descent through the cataract (see letter, 1854 ed., pp. 156–57). At Kalabsha, there is a tem-

Hermes Trismegistus, to whom Nightingale refers in these
entries, refers to Thoth, the Egyptian god of wisdom, whom the
Greeks identified with Hermes, and called the 'thrice-great' *(trismegistus)*. A body of philosophical and occult texts, collectively
known as the *Hermetica*, were attributed to him during the
Graeco-Roman period, and for centuries the texts were believed
to predate Moses, Pythagoras, and Plato. It was not until the sev-
enteenth century that the texts were correctly dated to the late
first to third centuries A.D. Although the texts incorporate elements of Platonic, Stoic, and Judaic philosophy, it has been
demonstrated in recent years that they are equally consistent
with ancient Egyptian theology as well.[32] Certainly Nightingale
believed that they were representative of Egyptian thought, as
judged by her letters.

Although lacking a single dogma or scriptural canon, the
philosophical *Hermetica* express a passionate piety, a craving for
the deliverance from the tyranny of Fate, for the knowledge *(gnosis)* and understanding of God, identification with Him, and in the
end immortality by union with the One.[33] The strong mystical elements of the *Hermetica* appealed greatly to Nightingale as at-
tested by the frequent references to Hermetism in her letters from
Egypt.[34] In one of them, Nightingale quoted at length from *Pimander*, a hermetic text that describes the origin of the cosmos
and the creation of man. Pimander, "the Mind of the Sovereignty"
(Sovereignty = God), reveals to Hermes Trismegistus the origins
of the cosmos from a watery abyss, reminiscent of Genesis I, but
even more similiar to the primordial waters of Nun in the Egyptian tradition. Out of this darkness is born light (= Mind), and from
the light emanates the Word (Logos), the 'son of God.' The Word
then establishes order out of the primeval chaos.

---

ple built by Augustus, and at Beit el-Wali, a rock-cut temple built by Rameses II.

32. Erik Iversen, *Egyptian and Hermetic Doctrine* (Copenhagen: Museum Tusculanum Press, 1984).

33. H. Idris Bell, *Cults and Creeds in Graeco-Roman Egypt* (Chicago: Ares, 1985
reprint), p. 75.

34. The 1854 edition of Nightingale's *Letters from Egypt* contains more references to hermetic philosophy than does Anthony Sattin's edition.

Mind, comprising both male and female within itself (as is the case with the Egyptian god Atum), is able to procreate and thus produces another Mind, the 'Maker of things,' the Demiurge. As Mind the Maker and the Word are of the same substance, both having arisen from Mind the Father, they unite. In doing so, however, the Word soars up and away from the coarser elements of creation, thereby depriving the natural world of reason. Man, to the contrary, arises from Mind the Father, who is light and life, and thus is endowed with an immortal principle. Although spiritual in his origin, when Man falls in love with Nature, he goes to dwell in matter that is "devoid of reason." Pimander concludes his discourse on cosmogenesis with the adage that if man could but know himself, he would discover his true divine nature and have eternal life. Noting the biblical parallels, Nightingale explained that:

> the *Father of all*, who is the *light and the life*, created man *after His likeness*, and received him as His son, and being pleased with man *in His own image*, gave him power over His works
> (And God saw everything that he had made, and behold, it was very good; and He gave man to have dominion over the fish of the sea, &c. &c.)
> Man then "falls into slavery," God warning him "that the love of the earthly part of himself shall be the cause of his death."
> "He then who knows himself, wins the good superior to himself;" and, "he who lets himself be deceived by the love of the body, is thrown into the shadow of death." "God, who is wisdom, wills that every man, who has part in His wisdom, should know himself."[35]

Pimander then proceeds to describe the means for entering into eternal life. Following the dissolution of the material body, "the senses go back into their own sources, becoming parts of the universe, and entering into fresh combinations to do other work." This, of course, suggests reincarnation to which Nightingale refers in her "Visions of Temples" (see Part II). The spirit, however, as-

---

35. *Letters from Egypt* (1854 ed.), letter of February 1850, pp. 225–27. (This passage is not included in Sattin's edition of the letters.)

cends through the heavenly spheres to the presence of God, actually entering *into* God. Nightingale expounds upon this in her letters in order to present her own view that it is through trial and tribulation that humanity is made perfect:

> In that dialogue of Hermes Trismegistus between Pimander and Thoth, he says what truth is. The soul went through several mystic regions before it began again the course of its transformations — those transformations, which only meant the trials, the stages which the divine emanation has to go through before arriving at perfection.

Noting the presence of the perennial philosophy in all faiths, at the conclusion of her discussion, she exclaimed:

> How like to one another are the highest beliefs in all spiritualised nations; and how much I find in Hermes Trismegistus of what — — — used to say to me!

With its emphasis on *gnosis* and self-knowledge as a means of knowing God, the *Hermetica* are not unlike the contemporary Christian gnostic scriptures that combined elements of Judaism, Christianity, and more ancient traditions. Gnosticism was also of interest to Nightingale, and thus she urged her friend Julius von Mohl, a German orientalist, to write a book on the Gnostics "whose idea was, as you say, a sort of quintessence of the idea of all the other Religions."[36] (At this time, gnosticism was known chiefly through the vituperations of the Church Fathers, and a work written by German theologian F. C. Baur titled *Die Christliche Gnosis*, published in 1835. The bulk of Gnostic texts comprised by the Nag Hammadi Codices were not discovered until 1945.) Nightingale's interest in Hermetism and gnosticism are indicative of her interests in a more syncretic religion that combined elements of late pagan and Christian theology. Later in 1869 she wrote:

> I like the books of the early centuries of this Millennium . . . because they seem to me to rise so much higher

---

36. BM Add. MSS. 46,385.f.17.

than those, whether Protestant or R. Catholic or Ratio-
nalist of these later centuries, in the appreciation of how
this life is only a little piece of an eternal education. And
they often took pains to show that, if one's state of mind
is in conformity with this, what does the loss of all the
sacraments in the world signify — or sudden or early
death or loss of opportunities or &c. &c.?[37]

It appears, however, that she would never reconcile herself to the
'lost opportunities.'

22. Tuesday
Put my two poor little chameleons ashore at Taphis. I was so
afraid of their following their comrade's example — so sorry to
part with them — they were such nice company.
    Went on shore at Dabod to see the 3 Pylons. Only Roman.[38]
    Sate long in the cold moonlight on the deck watching our
approach to Philae [figs. 10–11] & preparing myself for it.
Moonlight walk on the island. Sitting on Philae by the temple of
Isis with the roar of the Cataract I thought I should see *Him* [i.e.
Christ]. *His* shadow in the moonlight in the Propylaeum.

    Like Abu Simbel, the theology conveyed by the worship of
the goddess Isis at Philae appealed to Nightingale's spiritual dis-
position. According to Egyptian myth, Osiris was a beneficent king
of Egypt who was murdered and dismembered at the hands of his
brother Seth, and subsequently resurrected by his faithful wife Isis.
The resurrection of Osiris signified the regeneration of all life in
the cosmos, from the spiritual rebirth of an individual after death
to the annual inundation of the Nile and the regrowth of plants in
the spring. With its elements of death and resurrection, the myth

---

37. BM Add. MSS. 45,845.f.26.
38. Originally built in the third century A.D., the temple of Dabod received additions under the Ptolemies as well as Roman emperors Augustus and Tiberius. In
the 1960s, the temple was presented as a gift to Spain and moved to Madrid.

of Osiris thus provided an obvious parallel to the passion of Christ as Nightingale related to her family:

> I never *loved* a place so much — never felt a place so homey: thank God for all we have felt and thought here. Every moment of that precious week, from before sunrise to long after moonlight had begun, I spent upon the Sacred Island, most of it in Osiris' chamber. . . .
>
> I cannot describe to you the feeling at Philae. The myths of Osiris are so typical of our Saviour that it seemed to me as if I were coming to a place where He had lived — like going to Jerusalem; and when I saw a shadow in the moonlight in the temple court, I thought, "perhaps I shall see him: now he is there."
>
> The chamber of Osiris was like the place where *He* was buried; and after our little service on the Sunday morning, I went and sat there, and I thought I had never sate in any place so sacred, nor ever could, except in Syria.[39]

23. Wednesday

At sunrise we were on Philae & discovered the Chamber of Osiris.

Lewis's there.[40] Went to Osiris' Chamber — staid there till 3 o'clock. Mr. & Mrs. Lewis dined with us. Cold moonlight walk on Philae.

---

39. Letter of January 28, 1850, *Letters from Egypt* (1854 ed.), p. 160.

40. John Frederick Lewis (1805–76), British painter of Italian, Spanish, and Eastern subjects who traveled to Egypt in 1842. He returned to England in 1851 and subsequently became president of the Water-colour Society. In a letter to her parents, Florence wrote of the Lewises:

> He is making a series of drawings of the temple of Isis, and is a picture himself; he always wears the Turkish dress — a blue gubbeh, white kaftan, red turban, and a long white beard: his wife, a nice little woman, young and pretty, always sits by him. (letter of January 28, 1850, Letters from Egypt, 1854 ed., p. 162).

When writer William Thackeray visited his friend Lewis in Cairo, he too was struck by how 'orientalized' Lewis had become. (See his *From Cornhill to Grand Cairo*.)

24. Thursday
While we were in the Sacred Chamber, Northampton party
disturbed us[41] — but we stuck to it and were there almost all
day.
        Surprised there by a man asking for baksheesh. Our Passion
Week.

25. Friday
Went over to Bidji — up the rocks to a burying ground in a
solitary basin at the top of the island — so wild, but not
desolate — & down to a palm tree oasis, a happy valley & deep
green Tara of the Nile on the other side — walked to Padre
Ryllo's[42] church on the main land. Osiris chamber. Dinner at
Lewis's at Mahatta by moonlight.

26. Saturday
Went with Mrs. Lewis to see Zehnab & her swimming aunt on
Bijji[43] — dear huts — & walked over the island with a party — how
different it looked. But yesterday I spoiled it all with dreaming.
Disappointed with myself & the effect of Egypt on me — Rome
was better.

    During her stay in Rome, secure in a convent surrounded
by the familiar images of Christianity with the Madre Santa
Columba as her spiritual director, Nightingale was apparently
at peace with herself and the world, however briefly. Throughout her Egyptian travels, however, she seems to have struggled

---

41. Later in Aswan, she wrote of the Northampton party: ". . . there was such a
'ruck' of English boats there — all the Northampton party, and a thousand others —
and nothing to eat, for they had devoured everything like locusts, even all the rice
and milk of Syene, that we turned savage and sailed before sunrise." (Letter of January 28, 1850, Letters from Egypt, 1854 ed., p. 169.)
    42. Padre Ryllo, a priest of Santa Trinita de Monti in Rome and acquaintance of
the Madre Santa Columba, was martyred in Abyssinia.
    43. Zehnab was a friend of Mrs. Lewis, "a child of four years old, the daughter
of a widow of sixteen. Zehnab's aunt, of ten, who is just married, and who showed
us her house with great pride, the nicest in the island, swam over to see Mrs. Lewis
at Mahatta this morning: every body swims here." (Letter of January 28, 1850, Letters from Egypt, 1854 ed., p. 164.)

to enjoy herself while dealing alone with her thoughts of a more meaningful existence, or what she called 'dreaming.' In Egypt, she would confront her 'demons' like the early Christian monks in their desert hermitages. The ancient monuments, with their multifarious depictions of divinities, served only to reflect her own unsettled state of mind, challenging her with questions concerning the nature of God and her very own existence. Rather than purging such images from her mind as early Christian zealots had attempted to do by defacing the monuments, Nightingale meditated on the ancients' religion, incorporating elements of it into her own unusual and eclectic theology. In an act of homage to the ancient gods, she left her crucifix in the sanctuary of the temple at Philae. Disturbed by the poverty of the modern Egypt, she pondered the destiny of humanity, how great nations could rise to great heights and then fall into ruin. In contrast to sentiments expressed in her diary, she continued to write enthusiastically and copiously to her family about her travels.

27. Sunday
Took my crucifix up before breakfast to lay it in the sacred dust of the Chamber of Osiris. Prayers. Scrambled around the rocks on a beautiful warm morning to the south. True sunday morning. With Mr. Harris all the afternoon & his black daughter—[— — —] people.[44] They drank tea with us. Farewell moonlight walk. All night with my head out of window learning every line of the temples under the palms by heart.

---

44. Anthony Charles Harris was a British merchant based in Egypt and a collector of antiquities. Several important papyri bear his name. Selima, his adopted daughter who had been educated in England, inherited his collection of antiquities and sold it to the British Museum in 1872. She died in 1895. In her letter of January 28, 1850, Florence wrote:

Mr. Harris, to whom we had a letter, came the evening before we left, with his Abyssinian daughter, the child of an Abyssinian woman. I like her much; a really sensible nice girl—black. He is very learned and very queer. (*Letters from Egypt*, 1854 ed., p. 166)

28. Monday
Sailed before sunrise — Down the Cataract like a race horse —
only one & a little one. Asouan to breakfast. Rode up to
Mahatta — paid visits along the Cataract — like a scene in Capt.
Cook. Bought my bracelets. Did not go to Elephantina.
Mr. Murray in the evening.[45]

29. Tuesday
Sailed before sunrise from Asouan — such a beautiful calm
morning as I lay in bed with my head out of window. Wrote my
account of Philae.

30. Wednesday
Kom Ombo before breakfast[46] — rather stupid — writing about
Philae. Hadjar Silsileh at noon — walked along the quarries —
quite warm — Mr. B. went to all on both sides[47] — Σ and I staid at
home — writing till late at night.

31. Thursday
Temple at Edfoo early. Apolloinopolis Magna — only
Ptolemaic — some distance from shore. Saw the potter at his
wheel (Neph).[48] Got ahead at last with my Philae letter. Osiris &
Scarabaeus from Edfoo.

February

1. Friday
Rose up early in the morning. Saddled up our ass. Took our
young men & rode 3 miles along such a charming desert to a

---

45. Charles Augustus Murray was the British Consul-General in Egypt from 1846
to 1863. Florence and the Bracebridges spent time with him in Cairo, and Florence
availed herself of his library. (Letter of November 29, 1849, *Letters from Egypt*,
1854 ed., pp. 26 ff.)
46. The temple of Kom Ombo dates from the Ptolemaic and Roman periods and
was dedicated to the gods Haroeris (Horus the Elder) and Sobek, who is depicted as
a crocodile.
47. Spanning both banks of the Nile, the site of Gebel el-Silsila comprises ancient sandstone quarries (east bank) and shrines of the eighteenth and nineteenth
dynasties (west bank).
48. A reference to the ram-headed god Khnum (Neph in older versions), who is
depicted as creating individuals on a potter's wheel. The temple of Edfu, built under
the Ptolemies, was dedicated to the falcon-god Horus.

little lodge in the wilderness — a temple which did look like a place of worship.[49] Tomb of the Admiral.[50] Enormous walls of the old town — a square — 35 ft. thick — crude brick.

Row with Trout but luckily she had a tooth ache so I was spared saying anything that night. Finished at night "zusammen geschrumpft" my Hermes for Σ.[51]

2. Saturday
Esne — walked to the Temple — like the Portico of the Infernal Regions[52] — & to the Pacha's garden & to see the Pacha's blue silk bed. Storm of sand. Nile ran upside down — air a sand shower which moves. Trout very poorly & nurse-able. Finished at night my account of Osiris Chamber for Σ.

A central tenet of Nightingale's spirituality is the belief that God does not rule the universe capriciously, but rather that the universe functions according to immutable laws (including, but not restricted to, scientific and mathematical laws) that were nothing more than the thoughts of God made manifest. In *Suggestions for Thought*, Nightingale recalled the sandstorm mentioned earlier to illustrate her point:

> Now, we know that there was not one molecule of sand
> or water in that confused whirlwind, which was there
> by chance, which had not a sufficient cause, so to speak,
> for occupying the place which it did, which was not

---

49. A reference to the temple of Hathor and Nekhbet built by Thuthmosis IV and Amenhotep III. In a letter she wrote of the trip to Eilethyia (el-Kab):

In this vast valley we found a 'lodge in the wilderness,' a little chapel built by Amunoph III. . . . Here the people must have come out from Eilethyia for evening sacrifice; and it looked like a place of worship, so still and holy, sitting on its little platform. (Letter of February 3, 1850, *Letters from Egypt*, 1854 ed., p. 171.)

50. The Tomb of Ahmose, son of Ebana, a military officer of the early eighteenth dynasty.
51. Ger., i.e., condensing her discussion of Hermes Trismegistus(?).
52. The temple of Esna was built under the Ptolemies, although the surviving structure dates from the Roman period (first to third centuries A.D.).

rigorously where it ought to be, according to the laws
or uniform rules of God.[53]

3. Sunday
Bitter night. Paolo: "18 days North wind—him Nile never done
this before. I freeze with cold—before I warm." Paolo
meditating. Wind too high to let us go on. Walked around the
town in a blinding whirlwind of sand & to the Temple.
Manufacturing centre of industry. Saw blue clothes.[54]

Thebes
4. Monday
Finished up all my letters. Arrived at Thebes at 12. Karnac.[55] Got
our letters from the Governor at Luxor.

5. Tuesday
Private tombs of Shekh Abd el Koorneh.[56]

6. Wednesday
Valley of the Kings.[57]

7. Thursday
Wrote home by Howard Galtons. Medina Tabou.[58] I was very
poorly & could only sit about.

8. Friday
Rameseum.[59]

---

53. *Suggestions for Thought* (Calabria & Macrae), p. 44.

54. Refers to the linen dyed blue and hanging across the streets (c.f. letter of February 3, 1850, *Letters from Egypt*, 1854 ed., p. 172).

55. Dedicated to the god Amun-Re, Karnak is the most extensive temple complex in Egypt. The principal structures date from the eighteenth to the twenty-fifth dynasties (ca. 1552–664 B.C.) (fig. 13).

56. Named for a Muslim saint, this area on the west bank of Luxor is known for its tombs of New Kingdom officials.

57. The valley containing the tombs of the kings of the New Kingdom (1552–1069 B.C.) (fig. 14).

58. Medinet Habu, the site of the mortuary temple of Rameses III.

59. The mortuary temple of Rameses II (fig. 15).

9. Saturday
Trout had her tooth broken—poor soul!

Sore throat prevented me going out—but also from doing any thing. But I had some pleasant company with Moses over Miss Martineau's Sinai.[60] I had no idea what a philosophical & sincere man he [i.e. Moses] was.

In the second volume of *Eastern Life* Harriet Martineau wrote at length on Moses as she journeyed through the desert en route to Mount Sinai. She spoke of the great wisdom he had learned from the Egyptians and how he attempted to initiate his people into the Egyptian mysteries, emphasizing above all the unity of the Divine. Whereas Martineau spoke of the important theological contributions Moses made in the spiritual history of humanity, Nightingale took a particularly *personal* interest in Moses, as evidenced by the references to him in her letters. To some extent she seems to have identified with Moses: as he was compelled to leave his Egyptian mother in order to do God's will, so did Florence feel compelled to leave her family to pursue her interests in nursing, which she deemed to be God's will. As Moses led his people into a new covenant with God, so would Nightingale attempt to lead her compatriots to a better understanding of God with her *Suggestions for Thought*. Writing about Moses to her family, she almost seems to be describing herself and her relationship with her own mother with whom she had been at odds:

> To-day I walked with Moses, under the palms. . . . How grieved he must have been to leave Memphis,—guilty of ingratitude, as he must have seemed, towards his princess-mother, who had so tenderly and wisely reared him, and given him the means of learning all he valued so much, as the way of raising his brethren. . . . I do not know any man in all history with whom I sympathize so much as with Moses—his romantic devotion—his disappointments—his aspirations, so much higher than

---

60. Refers to Harriet Martineau's *Eastern Life: Past & Present.*

anything he was able to accomplish, always striving to give the Hebrews a religion they could understand.[61]

While in Egypt, Nightingale retraced the steps of both Moses and Plato [see March 21]. Although she regarded highly Platonic philosophy, she admired the *active* role that Moses personally played in shaping the destiny of his people:

> Moses was the greater man; for whereas Plato only formed a school, which formed the world, Moses went straight to work upon the world ("as if a God had been abroad, and left his impress on the world"), the chisel as it were to the block,... he was not only the sculptor, but the workman of the statue, the scholar, the gentleman, and the hard-working man, all in one.[62]

These remarks are very similar to those made by Harriet Martineau in her *Eastern Life,* where she also compared Moses and Plato: "Moses redeemed a race of slaves, made men of them, organised them into a society, and constituted them a nation; while Plato did only theoretical work of that kind..." (I, 172–73).

10. Sunday
In bed — but made some use of my day as a pause in this spiritual and intellectual whirlwind.

11. Monday
Did not go out — but the demon of dreaming had possession of my weakened head all the morning. Wrote a little letter for the American boat but could not do much.

12. Tuesday
Medineh Taboo. Wrote by the steamer.

---

61. Letter of March 18, 1850, *Letters from Egypt,* 1854 ed., pp. 259–60.
62. Letter of Palm Sunday, 1850, ibid., p. 284.

In the latter part of February, references to Nightingale's unsettled state of mind become more frequent. She continues to be troubled by 'dreaming,' she again hears the voice of God calling to her, and she vividly recalls the words of her 'madre' Santa Columba, abbess of the convent in Rome where she went on retreat in March of 1848. The situation continues to intensify in the following months with episodes of utter despair alternating with resignation and joy. Yet, Nightingale revealed very little of this situation to her family. The only indication of her true state of mind is the lengthy philosophical and theosophical expositions she continued to write to them.

Nightingale was an ardent student of comparative religion and philosophy, which undoubtedly contributed to her unorthodox religious views later detailed in *Suggestions for Thought*. In addition to her interest in ancient Egyptian religion, Hermetism, gnosticism, and Christianity, she became familiar with the teachings of Islam, Sufism, Hinduism, and Buddhism. During her trip she frequently compared Egyptian beliefs and inconography with those of Christianity. At Medinet Habu, she wrote:

> If there is one thing that strikes you more than any other, it is what would be called "Scriptural authority" for everything in the temples of Egypt. One seems to be positively reading the Old and some parts of the New Testament — viz., the Book of Revelations. There is the tabernacle of the Jews carried by the priests along the wall in the inner pronaos of the Ramesseum, only that there are four tabernacles; there are the cherubim of Ezekiel, with two wings stretched upward, and two covering their bodies, sitting upon the sacred ark at Medinet Tabou; and as to the four Evangelists, the Egyptian would find himself as much at home under the dome of St. Peter's, or in the Book of the Revelations, as I do at Medina Tabou. There is the ox of St. Luke, the lion of St. Mark, the eagle — no, not the eagle, it is a vulture or a hawk, and the Egyptian might as well march into St. Peter's, and seeing the gigantic Evangelists under the dome, pronounce the Christians guilty of the

most idolatry, deifying four biographers under the
symbols of beasts! as we utter the same accusation
against the worshippers of Medina Tabou.[63]

13. Wednesday
Dayr el Medeeneh (little Ptolemaic Temple) & Valley of the
Queens.[64]
    2 Murrays dined & Herr Koch came in.[65]

14. Thursday
Dayr el Bahree tombs — one Assaseef
                    — Koorneh Murrace
                    — Shekh Abd el Koorneh[66]
                    (nos 16, 17 destroyed by Lepsius)
    Rameseum — such a setting sun. Copied Koch's book.
Benczik came in for the evening.

15. Friday
Karnak.

16. Saturday
Karnak — & where was I? all the while that I was on Propylon, &
half the afternoon, dreaming. Karnak itself cannot save me
now — it has no voice for me.

---

    63. Letter of February 12, 1850, ibid., pp. 217–18. (This passage not in Sattin's
edition.)
    64. Contains the tombs of the queens and royal children of the New Kingdom.
    65. For Mr. Murray, see note 71. In a letter to her parents (BM Add. MSS 45,790,f.4),
Florence wrote of

> the little Koch, whom I am afraid you will not like, because he speaks,
> little but German — but he is cram-full of information, did everything
> for us — & we had not even a knife to give him in return. Pass him on
> to the Costers, if they will be kind to him — & if he is not too shy for
> them, to the Nicholsons — & be sure you give him something pretty
> & useful when he goes away for us, for he is poor.

    66. Assaseef, Koorneh Murrace, and Shekh Abd el Koorneh all designate areas
of the west bank of Luxor (fig. 12).

17. Sunday
Saw Lady Alford's drawings[67] & climbed into the Luxor sacred
place.[68]

18. Monday
Tombs of the Kings with Σ no 17. Sethos I. Ugly day. Did not
stop at Goorna.

19. Tuesday
Tombs of the Kings without Σ with Trout
   no 1. Rameses IX
      16 Rameses I earliest stopped-up
      17 Sethos I (Belzoni's)[69]
      11 Rameses III (Bruce's)[70]
       9 Rameses V
   took up Σ at Koorna.

20. Wednesday
   Rameseum
a [tomb] in the Asaseef — filled up
Shekh Abd el Koornah
   no 11
     35 again[71]
   Rameseum. Rode to Ptolemaic Temple of Medina Tabou &
then all round the Lake of the Dead, to the unburied & rejected
bodies on the other side.[72]

---

67. Lady Marian Alford (1817–88), artist and art patron, elder daughter of Spencer
Compton, second Marquis of Northampton. Florence was quite struck by her tal-
ent and remarked that "her genius is really Homeric" (*Letters from Egypt*, p. 215).
   68. I.e., the sanctuary of the temple of Luxor, built by Amenhotep III and Rameses II.
   69. Giovanni Battista Belzoni (1778–1823), Italian explorer and controversial collector whose archaeological finds formed the basis of the British Museum's Egyptian collection. In 1817, Belzoni discovered the spectacular tomb of Seti (or Sethos) I.
   70. James Bruce, a Scottish explorer who visited the Valley of the Kings in 1768
on his way to Ethiopia to find the source of the Nile. The tomb of Rameses III became known as 'Bruce's Tomb' since he copied and published scenes from the tomb.
   71. The tomb of Rekhmire, vizier of Thuthmosis III.
   72. A reference to Birket Habu, a large artificial lake excavated by Amenhotep
III (1390–52 B.C.). In her letters she described an area of exhumed burials "strewed
with whitened bones of men—little depressions shewing in the sand where once
they had been buried" (*Letters from Egypt*, 1854 ed., p. 212).

21. Thursday
Karnak. Our last day. 3 Propyla. Great Hall [fig. 16]. Rode around. View
of the Great Hall from temple of Sabaco. Rode round the little lake.

22. Friday
Luxor before breakfast. Long morning by myself at Old Koorna.
Sat on steps of Portico, moving with the shadow of the sun and
looking at that (to me) priceless view. God spoke to me once
again. Bade farewell to Rameseum, Medina Tabou, Colossi[73] like
gold in sunset for our last day.

Koorna is the site of Seti I's (or Sethos') mortuary temple
(fig. 17). Nightingale was struck by the beauty of this temple, and
wrote poetically of it to her family:

> Upon the steps of the colonnade I have sate for hours,
> moving with the shadow of the columns, as it turned
> with the sun, and looking out upon that matchless view
> under the different lights; the distance to the west over
> the green corn fields — then the palm garden — then the
> eastern hills on the other side the river — then more palms,
> and between their stems, the great colonnade of Luxor
> on its promontory, which becomes higher and higher, as
> the Nile sinks rapidly, and which one night was like a
> colonnade of chrysophrast shafts in the sunset. . . .[74]

Without revealing to them the mystical experience she had there,
she confessed that it was the only place in Thebes for which she
really cared.

During the month of February Nightingale wrote to her family no less than ten letters — on February 3, 4, 6, 10, 11, 12, followed by two undated letters, and then again on February 25 and
27. After her letter dated February 27, she would not write home
again until March 9 — a conspicuous interim of ten days. The rea-

---

73. Refers to the so-called 'Colossi of Memnon,' which once marked the entrance
to the mortuary temple of Amenhotep III.
74. *Letters from Egypt* (1854 ed.), pp. 206–7.

son for this interruption becomes apparent from the diary: God spoke to her again during this period (February 28) as she grappled with her call to service.

23. Saturday
Sailed for Kourneh — they went up to Valley of Kings. Farewell to Thebes. Wrote my letters. Sailed at 4 P.M.

24. Sunday
Keneh by dawn. They went to Dendera.[75] I tried to write but could not.

25. Monday
Sent letters by Consul. Mr. B. & I went to Dendera. Sailed at sunset.

26. Tuesday
Began writing up my notes.[76]

27. Wednesday
Made How before breakfast (Diospolis Parva). Rode to the tomb a mile into the desert (destroyed?).[77] All the afternoon in sight of How factory sugar chimneys.

28. Thursday
Walked around a civilized little village inland with village green & acanthus. Paolo had his fall. Hard at work with Tombs of the Kings.
God called me with my Madre's words.

---

75. Site of the Ptolemaic temple of the goddess Hathor.

76. I believe these notes to be the basis of what would become *Suggestions for Thought* (1860), a 65-page proof of which she completed in 1852. (See introduction, p. 7.)

77. She indicates in a letter that "we found the tomb we came to see positively carried away bodily, — the stones, the painted stones, gone to make a sugar-factory at How, where Mr. Bracebridge saw them afterwards" (letter of February 27, 1850, *Letters from Egypt*, 1854 ed., p. 251).

Nightingale first became acquainted with the Madre Santa Columba when she tried to place a little girl in the madre's orphan school in Rome. Once accepted into the school the child was personally provided for with an annual sum paid by Nightingale herself. The nun soon became Nightingale's confidante and spiritual director, and as we see in the diary, of lasting influence. Above all, Santa Columba stressed obedience to God's will. Nightingale must have told her about her family problems judging from the nun's admonition:

> It is no good separating yourself from people to try and do the will of God. That is not the way to gain his blessing. What does it matter even if we are with people who make us desperate? So long as we are doing God's will, it doesn't matter at all.[78]

After her retreat Nightingale recorded the conversation with her madre:

Santa Columba: Did not God speak to you during this retreat? Did he not ask you anything?
Nightingale: He asked me to surrender my will.
Santa Columba: And to whom?
Nightingale: To all that is upon the earth.
Santa Columba: He calls you to a very high degree of perfection. Take care. If you resist, you will be very guilty.[79]

March

1. Friday
Made Balsam.

---

78. O'Malley, p. 144.
79. O'Malley, pp. 144–45. The location of these notes is now unknown. They have not been found among Nightingale's papers in the British Library or in the Nightingale archive at Claydon House, Buckinghamshire.

Oh! My Madre, my Madre — this was the time I made the retreat with you which you said was more for me than for the children — two years ago.

Boat a hospital.[80]

Gave up Abydos.[81]

2. Saturday

At anchor opposite Girgeh all day — made it at night.

3. Sunday

Girgeh

Did not get up in the morning but God gave me the time afterwards, which I ought to have made in the morning — a solitary 2 hours in my own cabin, to "meditate" on my Madre's words.

4. Monday

Girgeh

5. Tuesday

Sailed 4 A.M.

Ekhmim (Panopolis)

Souhadj

6. Wednesday

Sailed 6 A.M.

Anchored under Gebel Shekh Hereedee.

7. Thursday

Gale all night & all day. Lying under Gebel Hereedee. God called me in the morning & asked me "Would I do good for Him, for Him alone without the reputation."

---

80. This reference is unclear. Perhaps several people on board were ill, although there are no references in her letters to this. It is also possible that Nightingale was envisioning the boat as a hosiptal as she often envisioned her home at Embley Park a hospital.

81. Her letter of March 9 indicates that a "north wind blowing like a tempest" prevented their stopping at Abydos, one of ancient Egypt's most sacred sites.

8. Friday
Thought much upon this question. My Madre said to me Can
you hesitate between the God of the whole Earth & your little
reputation? as I sat looking out on the sunrise upon the river in
my cabin after dinner.

9. Saturday
During half an hour I had by myself in the cabin, while Trout
[— — —] was up at Osyoot with Mustafa's[82] womans [sic], (till I
was called to advise Paolo about staying or going). Settled the
question with God.

10. Sunday
Every day, during the ¼ of hour I had by myself, after dinner &
after breakfast, in my own cabin, read some of my Madre's
words — Can you give up the reputation of suffering much &
saying little, they cried to me.

11. Monday
Thought how our leaving Thebes which was quite useless owing
to this contrary wind (we might have had another fortnight
there) but without it I might not have had this call from God.

12. Tuesday
Very sleepy. Stood at the door of the boat looking out upon the
stars & the tallmast in the still night against the sky (we were at
anchor — they were all asleep & I could not go to bed) & tried to
think only of God's will — & that every thing is desirable only as
He is in it or not in it — only as it brings us nearer or farther from
Him. He is speaking to us often just when something we think
untoward happens.

13. Wednesday
Made great way with the S. wind & great way with my Theban
letters too. Champollion[83] from the mad Count [Benczik] a great
help — wish we had him at Thebes.

---

82. The boat's cook.
83. Jean François Champollion (1790–1832), French Egyptologist who deciphered
Egyptian hieroglyphs in 1822. (He was also an acquaintance of Nightingale's friend,

14. Thursday
Finished my letters home in the morning & sate talking to
Σ & reading Pyramids all the afternoon, while Mr. B. was
on board the Harris boat, & we were beating about in the
wind.

15. Friday
Such a day at Memphis & in the desert of Sakkara [fig. 18] — &
God has delivered me from the great offense — & the constant
murderer of my thoughts.

16. Saturday–17. Sunday
Tried to bring my will one with God's about Athens & Malta
all the way as we rode in to Cairo. Can I not serve God as
well in Malta as in Smyrna, in England as at Athens? Perhaps
better — perhaps it is between Athens & Kaiserswerth —
perhaps this is the opportunity my 30th year was to bring
me. Then as I sat in the large dull room waiting for the
letters, God told me what a privilege he had reserved for me,
what a preparation for Kaiserswerth in choosing me to be
with Mr. B. during his time of ill health & how I had
neglected it — & had been blind to it. If I were never thinking
of the reputation, how I should be better able to see what
God intends for me.

18. Monday
Wrote home about Memphis & Fostat during the Khamsin[84] & to
Catherine Stanley about her marriage.

19. Tuesday
Great Pyramid [fig. 19]. Gave me no one impression.

20. Wednesday
Our last day in the boat. Packed up in a Khamsin i.e. in a
perspiration.

Christian von Bunsen.) The reference is probably to Champollion's *Précis du Sys-
tème Hiérogylphique* (1824).
  84. A hot, southerly wind that blows for a period of some fifty days.

21. Thursday
Left the boat wringing our hands. Such a delicious hour in the
gardens at Heliopolis — where Plato walked and Moses
prayed — undisturbed by my great enemy. Thought as we rode
home, how many who came the same road, would not have
planned how to surprise her husband by how ill she was but
how well.

In the course of her diary Nightingale uses language to describe her relationship to God that is not unlike the mystics of
medieval Europe — that is, she speaks of a mystical marriage with
God. This is suggested in the last line of the previous entry in
which she seems to be indicating that she should demonstrate to
her 'husband' (i.e., God) her strength rather than her weakness.
Later, on June 10, she recorded that God said she would come to
think of him as her cousin Lizzie thought of her husband. In the
language of mystics, marriage to God or Christ is an often-used
metaphor to express the desire of the soul ('the Bride') for a union
with God ('the Bridegroom'). Such a metaphor has scriptural basis
in the Song of Songs as well as in Isaiah (62:5), where marriage
signifies the relationship between God and His people, and in the
Gospels, where Jesus signifies the bridegroom (Matt. 9:15; Mark
2:19; Luke 5:34; John 3:29). Franciscan tertiary Angela of Foligno
(ca. 1248–1309) described the soul's desire for union with God in
passionate terms:

> Discovering that God is good, the soul loves him
> for his goodness. Loving him, it desires to possess him;
> desiring him, it gives all that it has and can have, even
> its own self, in order to possess him; and in possessing
> him, the soul experiences and tastes his sweetness. Pos-
> sessing, experiencing, tasting God himself, the supreme
> and infinite sweetness, it enjoys him with the greatest
> delight.[85]

---

85. *Angela of Foligno: Complete Works*, Paul Lachance, trans. (New York: Paulist
Press, 1993), p. 301.

Benedictine nun, Gertrud the Great of Helfta (1256–1301/02), spoke in equally amorous tones: "Ah, Jesus, the one and only cherished of my heart, dulcet lover . . . O flowering spring day filled with life, the amorous desire of my heart sighs and languishes. . . ."[86] As a nun and thus a consecrated 'Bride of Christ,' St. Teresa of Avila (1515–82) often referred to Christ as the 'Spouse:'

> He will teach you what you must do to please Him. Do not be foolish; ask Him to let you speak to Him, and, as He is your Spouse, to treat you as His brides. Remember how important it is for you to have understood this truth — that the Lord is within us and that we should be there with Him.[87]

Such a metaphor was used equally by male mystics. In his 'Spiritual Canticle,' St. John of the Cross described the longing of the bride (the soul) for her bridegroom (Christ):

> Where have you hidden,
> Beloved, and left me moaning?
> You fled like the stag
> After wounding me;
> I went out calling you, and you were gone.[88]

Nightingale was familiar with the works of these mystics and planned to incorporate their writings into an anthology titled *Notes from Devotional Authors of the Middle Ages* (ca. 1872) some of which had never been translated into English before.[89] Undoubtedly Nightingale's allusions to a spiritual marriage resulted from her knowledge of such writings, and her association with the Madre Santa Columba and other nuns.

---

86. Gertrud the Great of Helfta, *Spiritual Exercises*, Gertrud Jaron Lewis and Jack Lewis, trans. (Kalamazoo, Mich.: Cistercian Publications, 1989), pp. 42–43.

87. St. Teresa of Avila, *The Way of Perfection*, translated and edited by E. Allison Peers (New York: Doubleday, 1964), pp. 184–85.

88. *John of the Cross: Selected Writings* (New York: Paulist Press, 1987), pp. 221 ff. The same sentiment is expressed in his "Ascent of Mount Carmel," book 1, chapter 14.

89. BM Add. MSS 45,841.

22. Friday
Bade the last adieu to our dear boat & our men who came up to
see us & who cried at parting with us. Enjoyed the luxury of
having a room to myself for the first time — what use shall I
make of it?

23. Saturday
Knocking about all day — after the birds — & then to the
Citadel.

24. Sunday
Did not make any use of my Palm Sunday. Wrote letters till
midnight.

25. Monday
& then again from 6 o'clock. Bazar.

26. Tuesday
Spent much time at home reading my Madre's words.

28. Thursday
Looked out upon the silent city in the moonlight — & thought
what He would have done here — that great city, which cannot
discern its right hand from its left.[90]

29. [Good] Friday
Staid at home as knowing that I did not go to church to seek
God nor expect to find him there — read my Madre & my own
history. Did Christ thank God for this day when it dawned upon
him?

31. [Easter] Sunday
Sacrament.

---

90. C.f. *Letters from Egypt*, 1854 ed., (pp. 309–10): "And on the full moon of Holy
Thursday, as I looked out upon that vast city, which did not know its right hand
from its left. . . . I thought how Christ, if he had been there, would have felt; how
he would have yearned over Cairo, and how he would have been straitened till his
task was accomplished. Behold that great city—how would he have set about her
deliverance?" Nightingale is referring to remarks made by Jesus concerning the
fate of Jersusalem (Luke 19:41–44).

April

1. Monday
Not able to go out, but wished God to have it all his own way. I like Him to do exactly as He likes, without even telling me the reason why.

2. Tuesday
We all had to spend the night sitting up in that cabin of beasts. Found the prospect of having that wretched woman [i.e. Trout] to nurse cheer me up suddenly & all other woes grew light in comparison with hers.

3. Wednesday
Mme Rosetti[91] read her good book to us. Arrived at Alexandria.

5. Friday
Went to the externe school at S. Vincent de Paul. Mon Dieu, je lui dis toujours dans mes prieres. C'est votre affaire. Ce n'est pas la mienne. Je ne suis que cela dans vos mains—holding up the signal that she used in the school—(the nun)[92]

6. Saturday
The 3 orders at S. Vincent de Paul from Australia, Cairo, Alexandria—& the Hareem of Said Pasha.[93]

On her last day in Egypt, Nightingale went to say goodbye to the sisters of St. Vincent de Paul, and there she met the Reverend Mother of the Good Shepherd with whom she had spent time in

91. Madame Rosetti was the wife of the Consul for Tuscany in Egypt. Florence had made her acquaintance earlier in Cairo.

92. This entry is a puzzling combination of something Florence is saying to God: "'My God,' I say to him everyday in my prayers. 'It is your concern. It is not my own. I am only that in your hands'"; and a gesture made by a nun in the St. Vincent de Paul school in which she raised her hands as a signal for silence.

93. Said Pasha, the youngest son of Muhammad Ali, was to be the future viceroy, succeeding Abbas I in 1854. Nightingale described him as "an excellent man, an educated man, and a gentleman."

Cairo, as well as the Mother Superior of the Sisters of Mercy from Australia. After bidding farewell to the sisters, Nightingale was taken by Madame Rosetti to meet Engeli Hanum, the wife of Said Pasha.

On the afternoon of April 6, Nightingale and the Bracebridges set sail on an Austrian ship for Corfu. Although they had orignally planned to travel via Turkey, having learned of a British naval blockade of Piraeus near Athens, they decided to do their quarantine in Corfu where they would await further word of the political situation on the mainland. The blockade had been ordered by the British foreign secretary Lord Palmerston to support the claims of a British subject, Don Pacifico, against the Greek government. Pacifico, a Jewish merchant, had lost his property in anti-Semitic violence in Athens and had demanded restitution.

When Nightingale and the Bracebridges reached Corfu, however, they were informed by the master of the port that they would be unable to land for quarantine.[94] They were thus forced to continue on to Trieste, Ancona, and Brindisi in Italy, and then finally back to Corfu. Her letters continued to provide lengthy and eloquent descriptions of the journey, discourses comparing Egyptian and Greek philosophy, as well as forceful commentaries on the political situation in Italy and Greece. Much of Italy was still occupied by Austrian troops following the defeat of Napoleon. Clashes with Italian revolutionaries and nationalists had left their mark on cities like Ancona, which Nightingale described in a letter:

> Well, we went ashore at Ancona which we reached on Tuesday morning. Found the city shaken, the palaces burnt & broken, & bomb thro' the Duomo, where the people had taken refuge during the Austrian bombardment which lasted from March till June—a powder magazine blew up in consequence of a bomb, & the city looked as if it had been shaken by an earthquake. . . .[95]

---

94. BM Add. MSS 45,790.ff.2; letter to parents, Trieste April 15, 1850 (copy at Wellcome Institute).

95. Letter of April 20, 1850 (BM Add. MSS 45790.f.5.).

The British presence in Greece was a result of the Greek War of Independence (1821–32), whereby the country was wrested from the Ottoman Empire and placed under the protection of Britain, France, and Russia. With its proximity to the Ottoman and Russian empires, Greece was of significant strategic importance to Britain. Only four years after witnessing this delicate balance of power, Nightingale would find herself in the midst of a war waged by Britain, France and Turkey against Russia.

7. Sunday
In berth all day on board the Schild but passed a very happy day. My God, thy will.

8. Monday
In berth.

9. Tuesday
Passed Crete. Got up—had the very same wind which forced St. Paul out of his course from Alexandria.[96]

10. Wednesday
Mrs. Williamson[97] asked me why we avoided her. My God, do *I*, in all my intercourse (with Benczik, with Mr. Vernon, with Σ,

---

96. St. Paul did not actually sail from Alexandria, but rather in an Alexandrian ship that he boarded in Myra on the Lycian coast (Acts of the Apostles 27:6). The wind Nightingale refers to is the south wind which carried Paul's ship to Crete (Acts 27:13). In Athens, she would recall Paul again, remembering his speech before the Areopagus (Acts 17:19–31) (BM Add. MSS 45790.f15–29).

97. In a letter (April 20, 1850, BM Add. MSS 45,790, 3 ff.), Florence told her family about

> a certain Mrs. Williamson, an arrant flirt or something worse, whom we had been warned against at Cairo.... But the reason why I tell you this story is that she will claim us for acquaintances, perhaps make you act upon this claim. We avoided her constantly, steadily— & one day (I never dined down stairs) she came up upon the deck during dinner, sate down on my matress & asked me *why*—& I told her but *bonnement*. No one else on board would, & I thought it was not fair. I had not the pretension of thinking of reforming her. She cried very much, was determined to take no offense, was even civiller than before to both of us—but what did that matter! She was, if possible,

with her) consider only the object for which we are put into the
world — only the serving [of] thee.

11. Thursday
Could not stop at Corfu. But I only wish God to do His own will.
His will in every thing.

13. Saturday
Arrived at Trieste.

15. Monday
Sailed for Ancona.

16. Tuesday
Ancona. In my berth all the way to Brindisi.

18. Thursday
Brindisi. Slept on the floor of the gentlemen's cabin.

19. Friday
Corfu.

    Although the travelers had had an arduous voyage from Egypt,
Nightingale's thoughts continued to turn to spiritual questions.
Just as she described good and evil as the right and left hands of
God, so too did she couple joy with grief — perhaps alluding to her
own experiences in which true happiness was attained only after
enduring much suffering. In describing Corfu to her family, she
wrote:

> If you want a contrast to Egypt, it is here — the olives &
> orange trees, the most beautiful companions which God
> has created — they set off one another like Joy & Grief —
> for the olive tree is so strong in its one greatest associ-

---

more improper than before — & we held out to the last, tho nothing
could be more painful — we would have nothing to do with her & now,
if, she claims us, you know.

ation that it always reminds one & stands for the type of the greatest sorrow the world has yet seen — while the orange tree in all ages has been our type of Love & Joy. I never see its shining bright leaves & white blossoms against the dark olive, placed as Providence always has placed them together, without thinking of the Spirits of Good and Evil, & calling, tho' Isaiah has told me not, calling Evil good — for who shall say that the Evil of the Mount of Olives was not good?[98]

In her diary Nightingale also alludes to the Mount of Olives where Jesus agonized in prayer before his arrest: in Germany, she likened the Rhine to the Kedron, which flows by the Mount of Olives (July 31), and previously she had used language similar to that Jesus used while praying on the Mount of Olives (May 7). These references suggest that she identified with the suffering endured by Jesus.

Although she would spend the greater part of her life trying to alleviate suffering, Nightingale viewed suffering as an integral element in the evolutionary process in which humanity became one with God for it *revealed error*. Once the error had been identified and corrected, the suffering would be eliminated. This idea was central to her spiritual philosophy as later detailed in *Suggestions for Thought*, and was held in common by the medieval mystics whom she later translated for her *Notes from Devotional Authors*. The following passage by the Jesuit spiritual writer Jean Joseph Surin (1600–65), which was to have been included in the anthology, would have been particularly meaningful to her:

> One of the great misfortunes is not to make good use of our sufferings & infirmities of the body in which God has great designs for us, uniting Himself with the soul much more perfectly by pain & grief than by great consolations.[99]

---

98. BM Add. MSS 45,790 f.7.
99. BM Add. MSS 45,841.f60.

20. Saturday
Argostoli. Patras.

21. Sunday
Thanked God for the Turkish bath. Let me serve thee & thee
alone with the strength thou hast given me again.

22. Monday
Athens.

23. Tuesday
Turkish bath.

24. Wednesday
Thesieum[100] & dined at Mrs. Hill's.

Frances Hill was the wife of John Henry Hill (1791–1882), an
American businessman who became an Episcopal missionary. The
Hills established the first schools in Athens after the expulsion of
the Turks. After the Greek government established schools for
boys, the Hills devoted themselves to the education of girls. Their
school quickly acquired the reputation of being the best in Greece.
Respecting the traditions of the Greek Orthodox Church, the Hills
avoided teaching anything to the contrary and did not proselytize.
For thirty years, Hill also served as chaplain to the British Lega-
tion in Greece. The school founded by him and his wife continues
today as the Hill Memorial School. Mrs. Hill proved to be an important influence on Nightingale, as evidenced from the impas-
sioned diary entries in May and June, as well as from her correspondence. Nightingale admitted to Parthenope that she had not
seen much of Athens as she was spending most of her time with
the Hills, and wrote lovingly of them:

> I wish I could express what I feel for these dear people
> here. I never saw before any in the Protestant Church
> who had the real missionary in them, or if they were

---

100. The Temple of Hephaistos located in the Agora.

self-devoted, it was to some fid-fad or other, which they called "Scriptural principles," or "the Church," or "the truth" or some such nonsense, but of God & their *fellow-creatures* was not at all the question. . . .

As for Mrs. Hill, I never saw any body the least like her. She is the ideal of woman. I see in her the highest life which I believe can be led, on earth I will not say, for I believe she does God's will as it is in heaven — & therefore I suppose her, when I see her washing up the tea things, or giving her Bible lesson in the school, or teaching the Maids of Honour, to be already in heaven. And she is so like a child. What world they come from, I don't know. I never saw any thing like them here before for in my eyes their greatest glory is that they have not converted, in 20 years, one single soul. Their own words, when giving to a girl a copy of Archbp. Plato's Catechism, were, "that she might reverence the more the doctrines of her own Church in which we most earnestly desired her to remain." That is what I call a missionary — the rest are only theologians.[101]

In a letter to her Aunt Mai (Smith), Nightingale likened Mrs. Hill to another woman she greatly admired — her 'Madre' Santa Columba:

I am here in a missionary's house — a real missionary — not one "according to the use of the United Church of England" — but such as missionaries live in one's imagination — & it is interesting to me to see the "same mind as it was in Christ Jesus," clothed in a different coat, in different parts of the world — my Madre at Rome, whose mind was dressed in black & white nun's robes even more than her body — & the Evangelical American here, Mrs. Hill, my true missionary, are so alike — & both I see, are always listening for the voice of God, looking for his will.[102]

---

101. BM Add. MSS 45,790.f28–29.
102. BM Add. MSS 45793 f.75.

Nightingale recorded some of what Mrs. Hill related to her. As with her madre Santa Columba and with Mary Baldwin, another missionary she met in Athens (see later), Mrs. Hill emphasized the will of God as the guiding force in her life. She told Nightingale:

> When we had all the troubles which we have had here, if we had felt that we had come here of our own being, & not that God had sent us, we could not have borne them.
>
> But we moved no finger in the matter. We had neither act nor part in it — the way was opened for us to come here.
>
> If I had been told before I came where I was going to, the life I was going to lead here, the responsibility, I should have said, "It was impossible" — for I am unfit for it. Before I came here I had nothing at all to do — & I used to wish for something. I *did*, but when I thought of a missionary life, I did not know whether I could do it, you know.
>
> Then we came here, I did. I did the duty each day presented for me, & I left it to Providence to open the way I should follow.[103]

25. Thursday
Mrs. Hill's school — wonderful order. Rain.

26. Friday
Mrs. Hill's school. Walked around the back of the Acropolis [figs. 21 and 22], between Pnyx and Areopagus.

27. Saturday
Salamis & the British fleet.[104]

28. Sunday
Got my letters.

---

103. BM Add. MSS 43,402.f.39.
104. Refers to the blockade over the Don Pacifico incident (see p. 52).

29. Monday
[Temple of] Jupiter Olympius [fig. 24]. Moved to Mr. Hill's.

30. Tuesday
In the evening, while they [the Bracebridges] were at the
Wyses,[105] Mrs. Hill gave me the account of how she began her
missionary life. It was always God who made the initiative
never she. It was never her doing—always circumstances—only
to do the duty which offers itself for the day was the way, she
said. Let God show the way by his circumstances. Her beginning
the school again in '42. Wonderful silence in school she
considers necessary.

May

1. Wednesday
Mr. Wyse's. Am I here in the name of God?

4. Saturday
Turkish bath & on the bed all day.

5. Sunday
Took the Sacrament.

7. Tuesday–8. Wednesday
I have felt here like the suspension of all my faculties. I could
not write a letter. Could not read. Could not exert myself in
any way. But I am thankful for it—it teaches me to wait upon
the will & laws of God—that power of always writing a good
letter whenever one likes is a great temptation—it makes one
think all time wasted if one has not done that—God has now
taken away that power—that I may do every thing only for
the sake of doing His will. Lord, let me give everything to
thee.

---

105. Sir Thomas Wyse (1791–1862), politician and diplomat who was appointed
British Minister to Athens in 1849.

9. Thursday
I cannot even draw a pattern for many minutes without turning
faint — but "Mon Dieu, je vous ai tout donné." [106]

12. Sunday
To day I am 30 — the age Christ began his mission. Now no more
childish things, no more vain things, no more love, no more
marriage. Now, Lord, let me only think of Thy will, what Thou
willest me to do — O Lord, Thy will, Thy will. [107]

13. Monday
I have been reading Henry Martyn. "I see no business before me
in life but the work of Christ, neither do I desire any
employment to all eternity but his service" — Now they all
think only of God's will, of finding out what is His will for them
to do, this man, my Madre, Mrs. Hill, Mary Baldwin. [108]

15. Wednesday
Bewell[?] day.

16. Thursday
Bled in the foot. [109]
Made extracts from Henry Martyn.

---

106. "My God, I have given you all."
107. St. Catherine of Genoa who Nightingale read expressed similar sentiments,
exclaiming: "Oh Lord, no more world, no more sins!" (*Catherine of Genoa: Purgation & Purgatory, The Spiritual Dialogue.* New York: Paulist Press, 1979, p. 109).
Is this perhaps a case of 'unsconscious spiritual plagiarism'? Henry Manning, a
friend of Nightingale's wrote an introduction to a translation of Catherine's 'Treatise on Purgatory.'
Nightingale's exclamation is, of course, also similar to that of Jesus who prayed
on the Mount of Olives: ". . . yet not what I will, but what thou wilt." (Mark 14:36),
a passage that Nightingale marked in her own Bible.
108. Mary Baldwin, of Virginia, was a member of the Hill's household and school
staff, and someone who Florence admired.
109. In a letter to Parthenope (BM Add. MSS 45,790.f56 ff.) she described her
physical condition:

> As you may perhaps see Mr. Lyons in London, & he may tell you that
> he has not seen me, I think it best to state to the British public in my
> own hand that I have not been well since I came to Athens. I was a

The extracts Nightingale made from Martyn's *Memoirs*, found among her personal papers in the British Library,[110] illuminate her internal state during this period and are thus included here in their entirety. (Page numbers following the excerpts refer to Henry Martyn's *Memoirs*, 1858 edition).

I look back with pity & shame upon my former self, when I attached importance to my life & labours. [p. 308]

It is because I am *one with Christ* that I am so wounded. [p. 310]

Because we have the Spirit of the Father — what he wishes we wish: what he hates, we hate. [p. 311]

I could not be happy if God was not glorified & if I had not the enjoyment of his presence, for which I felt that I was now educating. [p. 315]

It is probable that the best world may be akin to this, & our relation to both not dissimilar. But here we see that childhood is a preparation for manhood, & that neglect of the proper employment of childhood entails miseries in riper years. [p. 318]

The angels in heaven were rejoicing at my being so soon to find a heavenly Father. [p. 17]

O Thou whose I am, no longer my own, once more would I resign this body & soul to the disposal of thy holy will. [pp. 47–48]

little knocked up with the fortnight at sea & it ended in a sort of low fever for which Mrs. Hill insisted on sending for her confidential Doctor & I was bled in the foot, told to drink a great deal of everything but medicine & eat no meat, by which treatment *à l'Orientale* I was able to go up to Penteticus on Saturday.

110. BM Add. MSS 43402 f.38. These extracts had been tentatively identified as notes of conversations with Mrs. Hill but are in fact extracts of Martyn's *Memoirs*. (Mrs. Hill's words follow the Martyn excerpts.)

I wish for no created good or for men to know my experience: but to be one with thee & live for thee. [pp. 94–95]

To have a will of my own, not agreeable to God's is a most tremendous folly: let me never dare to think of being dissatisfied. [p. 217]

I see *no business before me in life* but the work of Christ, neither do I desire any employment *to all eternity* but his service. [pp. 76–77]

I had rightfully no other business each day but to do God's work as a servant, constantly regarding his pleasure. [p. 78]

A despicable indulgence in lying in bed gave me such a view of the softness of my character that I resolved on my knees to live a life of more self denial. [p. 58]

The views of my own heart have produced, *not* humility but *discontent*. [p. 38]

I pass so many hours as if there were no God at all. [p. 38]

Setting a watch over my first thoughts on awakening in the morng, I find to be an excellent preparation for a right spirit during the day. [pp. 38–39]

What am I that I should *dare* to do my own will? [p. 40]

I like to find myself employed usefully, in a way I did not expect or foresee, especially if my own will is in any degree crossed by the work unexpectedly assigned me: as there is then reason to believe that God is acting. [pp. 307–8]

17. Friday
In four evenings Mary Baldwin has given me the history of her
coming here — She had no strong belief in her mission, no
presentiment, no conviction that this was her vocation — but to
take what was presented to her, to follow the indications of the
will of God & prepare herself for them, that was her mission —
that [was] her way.[111]

18. Saturday
Tomorrow will be Sacrament Sunday. I have read over all my
history, a history of miserable woe, mistake & blinding vanity,
of seeking great things for myself.

19. Sunday
Oh how happy I am to be away from the scene of temptation
on this day [Pentecost]. I thank thee, Father, three
Whitsuntides have I spent torn by temptation & overcome —
Here I am not safe — but at all events I am not adding the act to
the thought. God, I place myself in thy hands. Thy will is all
my desire — if it be thy will that I shall go on suffering hell, let
it be so — but let me only learn only to desire what Thou
desirest.

20. Monday
All the afternoon a voice was saying to me, *If thou knowest the
gift of God & who it is that saith unto thee, Give me to drink,
thou wouldst have asked of him, & he would give thee living
water*[112] — Lord, thou askest me to do thy will, & I am to ask of
thee life, life to do it for I am dead.

---

111. In her private notes, Florence recorded some of what Mary Baldwin had
related:

> I made it the subject of prayer for a week — the missionary pro-
> posal. I had never thought of being a foreign missionary, I thought
> that an honour too great for me — & I did not know whether I could
> do it. I made up my mind to do whatever my hand found to do. It
> was all offered to me. I made no steps of my own. (BM Add. MSS
> 43,402.f.40)

112. Nightingale is quoting Jesus' response to the Samaritan woman (John
4:10).

21. Tuesday–23. Thursday
I have not been able to see anything of Athens, but to come
here only to see & know these dear people was enough. If I had
offered ten times as much. The privilege of knowing them
must have been given me to turn me to the will of God — to
show me what was the true end of my life — not to be useful
nor to accomplish this or that mission, but to find out as they
do, what is the will of God for me. My Madre & Mrs. Hill, to
have known two such people. Now I am 30 — the year when I
thot [sic] I should have accomplished my Kaiserswerth
mission — but let me only accomplish the will of God. Let me
not desire great things for myself. Went to Allopiki with Mrs.
Hill. Suffered very much. A few words of love from her turned
all my thoughts to God. I was glad I had come merely to hear
them.

24. Friday–25. Saturday
God has brought me to Athens to teach me to look for His will.
This was His birthday present to me. Surely some great
temptation must be preparing, that this great privilege has been
granted me. This breathing time — if I had been all day long
seeing Athens, I should not have remembered my vows for my
30th year. I think that not seeing Athens would be the
preparation for my birth day — it has been so, but in a different
way — seeing something better at Athens.

26. Sunday
Resolved to devote ¼ of hour 3 times a day to finding out what
was the will of God for me.

27. Monday
Reading Cowper's life — his madness — or is *he* sane & is it we
who are mad? There is no one whom I feel such a sympathy for
as Cowper — his deep despondency, his earnest single
heartedness.

William Cowper (1731–1800) was one of the most widely
read English poets of the eighteenth century. Alternately tor-

tured and consoled by his religious convictions, Cowper suffered
bouts of mental illness and believed that he was predestined to
eternal damnation. In his own *Early Life of William Cowper*
(1817), he detailed his various attempts at suicide. Although
there is no evidence that Nightingale ever attempted suicide, it
has already been noted that she did in times of despair ask God
to *let* her die. She would repeat this sentiment in December of
1850 (see following). Nightingale's sympathy with Cowper is
clearly indicative of her own distressed spiritual and mental
state at this time. While her own spiritual convictions were often
a great comfort to her, she frequently believed that she was fail-
ing to serve God's purpose. In a letter to Parthenope (May 31,
1850), she quoted Cowper: "The path of sorrow & that path alone
leads to the land where sorrow is unknown."[113] In the same letter she described her visit to the cave of the Eumenides where
she

> sate & thought of poor Cowper's sufferings, but not bit-
> terly. I like to think how the Eumenides' laws work out
> all things for good & I would not be such a fool as to
> pray that one little [sic] of hell should be remitted, one
> consequence altered either of others mistakes or of our
> own. [The Eumenides (literally, 'well-minded ones') is
> a euphemism for the Furies, three terrible goddesses who
> pursue and punish evil-doers.]

Although her diary lacks entries between May 27 and June 4, she
continued to write to her family, occasionally providing a clue to
her own innermost thoughts. Comparing ancient Greek and Christian ideas, she wrote of progression through suffering:

> How proud the Greeks were—how anxious to avoid any
> low or common images, when they represented Athena
> Wisdom springing at once in full majesty & perfection
> from the Primeval Power. Yet I like our conception bet-
> ter—the conception by which our God passes through
> all the stages & humility of childhood—the slow growth

---

113. BM Add. MSS 45,790 f.56–70. The quote is from Cowper's "Epistle to an
Afflicted Protestant Lady in France."

by which he is made perfect thro' suffering is more really
sublime & certainly more true than of the sudden development of wisdom.[114]

June

4. Tuesday–9. Sunday
I thought I would go up to the Eumenides Cave & ask God
there to explain to me what were these Eumenides which
pursued me. I would not ask to be released from them —
Welcome Eumenides — but to be delivered from doing further
wrong. Orestes himself did not go on murdering. But
Tuesday & Wednesday I had a letter to copy for Mr. B. &
Thursday to go out in the carriage. Friday I sate before
breakfast & thought of my despair — this day twelve months
[ago], June 7, 1849 I made that desperate effort, that
Crucifixion of the sin, in faith that it would cure me. Oh
what is Crucifixion — would I not joyfully submit to
Crucifixion, Father to be rid of this. But this long moral
death, this failure of all attempts at cure. I am just in the
same state as I was last June 7. I think I have never been so
bad as this last week. When Plato's plane tree, when riding in
the Academy, when living intercourse with these dear Hills
could not recall my attention to actual things. And I thought
when I was 30, I should be cured. 8 months since the last
incentive to sin, & not a day has passed without my
committing it. I went & sate in the cave of the Eumenides
alone, & thought how they pursued me — & how would it
end? A wretched [sic] that I am. Who shall deliver me from
the body of this death? What does it signify to me now
whether I see this or do that or not? I never can be sure of
seeing it. I may see nothing but my own self practicing an
attitude. I shall be in just the same state June 7, 1851
according to human calculation as I am now.

---

114. BM Add. MSS. 45,790 f.74.

10. Monday
The Lord spoke to me: he said, Give five minutes every hour to the thought of me. Couldst thou but love me as Lizzie loves her husband, how happy thou wouldst be — in all situations. But Lizzie does not give five minutes every hour to the thought of her husband. She thinks of him spontaneously every minute. So also in time shalt thou do.

12. Wednesday
To Megara! Alas it little matters where I go — sold as I am to the enemy[115] — Whether in Athens or London, it is all alike to me.

13. Thursday
Half an hour of dark solitary silence at Mr. Wyse's — it was a moment of repose in the series of struggles, in which I am always worsted, of defeats under which I am sinking and dying.

17. Monday
After a sleepless night, physically & morally ill & broken down, a slave. Glad to leave Athens. I had no wish on earth but to sleep, an unbroken sleep in my little bed at Lea Hurst. There it seemed to me as if forgetfulness opened her mother's arms to me. There I wished to be, but only to sleep.

Nightingale and the Bracebridges were supposed to leave Athens on June 3, but the boat they were to take broke down. In the meantime, Nightingale continued to spend time alone with Mrs. Hill. They were finally able to book passage on an Austrian war steamer bound for Callimaki and departed on June 17. The Hills accompanied them as far as Corfu.

18. Tuesday
I had no wish to be on deck. I let all the glorious sunrises, the gorgeous sunsets, the lovely moon lights pass by. I had no wish,

---

115. I.e., 'dreaming.'

no energy. I longed but for sleep. My enemy is too strong for
me — every thing has been tried. Mrs. Hill's teaching, the beauty
of the East — all, all is in vain.

20. Thursday
Corfu.

21. Friday
Two delightful days at Corfu. My enemy let me go. I lived again,
both in body & mind. Oh! today, how lovely, how poetic it
was — & I was free.

22. Saturday
Off by the Levant boat. Gradual respite from animals delightful.
Began to sleep.

24. Monday
Writing home all the evening — & here too I was free.

25. Tuesday
A happy day at Trieste writing home.

29. Saturday
Four long days of absolute slavery — on the road from Trieste to
Vienna — in vain I called upon the shadows of Adelsberg to rise
up & exorcise me as they had done Albert.[116]

30. Sunday
I could not write a letter — could do nothing.

July

1. Monday
I lay in bed at night & called upon God to save me. My soul
spoke to His & I was comforted.

---

116. Probably refers to Saint Albert the Great (1193?–1280), a Dominican bishop
and philosopher, who was canonized in 1931 as the patron of the natural sciences.
Adelsberg, now Postojna in southwestern Slovenia, is known for its stalactite caves.

2. Tuesday
[— — —] not quite so bad.

3. Wednesday
How little I thought that I should have been at Prague & so
despairing, so helpless as I was to night — as I lay in bed
meditating [on] my utter hopelessness of relief, how lost I was &
past redemption, a slave that could not be set free.

4. Thursday
At Dresden why I don't know I felt relieved.

6. Saturday
I stood an hour before that Ecce Homo — it reflected my
feelings — it spoke despair — no hope — all had failed — And the
next Ecce Homo hoped. Why — it lifted up its eyes to God.[117]

7. Sunday
I took the Sacrament but why? I had no hope. I took it only as a
proof of sympathy with Christ's plans. I stood before the
Raphael — & thought that was what woman might be, was
intended to be.[118]

9. Tuesday–11. Thursday
A miserable week at Berlin — I did not think it worth while to
get up in the morning. What could I do but offend God? I never
prayed. All plans, all wishes seemed extinguished, And now, on
the brink of accomplishing my greatest wish, with Σ positively
planning for me, I seemed to be unfit, unmanned for it — it
seemed not to be the calling for *me*.

I had 3 paths among which to choose — I might have been a
married woman, a literary woman, or a Hospital Sister. Now it
seemed to me, as if quiet, with somebody to look for my coming
back, was all I wanted. I did not feel the spirit, the energy for

---

117. *Ecce homo*, Latin for "Behold, the man," the words Pontius Pilate spoke
when he presented the scourged and crowned Jesus to the crowd (John 19:5). That
Nightingale identified with such a scene is indicative of the great distress she was
experiencing at this time.
118. A reference to Raphael's 'Sistine Madonna' (fig. 26).

doing anything at Kaiserswerth. To search out the will of God
for me seemed so far from me. I could not do it.

15. Monday
To Bethanien — to the Library.[119]
    All at once I felt how rich life was. There was Mlle de
Rantzau's life[120] — there was the life of acquiring, among the
Mythology, the Philosophy of all nations' religions. The life of
Berlin struck me as so full & free & rich.

16. Tuesday
To the library for an hour — to the Deaf & Dumb [Institution],
but they were in Ferien [i.e. on holiday]. We heard a few however
speak remarkably well.
    To Bethanien, & dear Mlle de Rantzau took me to the
Infant Hospital, to see Mlle de Hochwächsen doing the same
thing herself (for love) at the Elizabeth Krankenhaus [hospital],
then brought me home & gave me coffee & her advice. 2 months
at K[aiserswerth,] two at Strasburg, 2 with her & was so kind.
My hopes revived. Wished Mr. Pertz goodbye.[121]

    The "Deaf & Dumb" mentioned here refers to the Institu-
tion for the Deaf established in 1788 by the son-in-law of Samuel
Heinicke, who had founded the first German public school for the
deaf in Leipzig ten years previously. Nightingale's interest in the
education of the deaf may have originated with Dr. Samuel Gridley Howe, an important figure in American education for the blind
and deaf, who visited the Nightingales in 1844 and advised Florence on a nursing career. She was also friends with Dr. Richard

---

119. Bethanien ("Bethany") was a deaconess hospital founded under the tutelage
of Kaiser Friedrich Wilhelm IV in 1847 with the assistance of Theodore Fliedner of
Kaiserswerth (see p. 78). The Library refers to the Royal Library.
    120. Marianne von Rantzau was the Superintendent of Bethanien. She had spent
a year of training at the Institution of Deaconesses at Kaiserswerth.
    121. Georg Heinrich Pertz (1795–1876), the chief librarian of the Royal Library
and the first general editor of the *Monumenta Germaniae Historica*. In a letter to
her mother (August 1853), she described him as a "perfect Encyclopedia & Library
in himself" (copy at the Wellcome Institute of the History of Medicine, London).
In 1853 he visited the Nightingales in England.

Fowler (1765–1863) of the Salisbury Infirmary (where Nightingale had hoped to train as a nurse), and author of *Some Observations On the Mental State of the Blind and Deaf and Dumb* (1843). During her trip to Rome in 1848 she had hoped to visit a boys' school for the deaf, but was prevented from doing so because of her gender.[122] She would also visit a school for the deaf in Belgium (see later).

After leaving Berlin, Nightingale traveled to Hamburg for a day purposely, it seems, to see Amalie Sieveking (1794–1859) whose address is written at the front of the diary. Sieveking was a friend of Christian von Bunsen's whom she visited in London, and thus it is possible that she met Nightingale there, or perhaps Bunsen told Nightingale of Sieveking's work with the poor and sick. Like Nightingale, Sieveking regarded service to her fellow man as a means of serving God. Motivated by fervent religious beliefs, she helped found a school for poor girls in Hamburg. When a cholera epidemic hit Hamburg in 1831, she volunteered for hospital service, where she assumed superintendence of the wards. Soon after, she established a society for the care of the sick and poor, designed to meet their material and spiritual needs not met by municipal agencies. In 1840 she founded the 'Amalienstift,' which comprised a children's hospital and living quarters for the poor.[123] Pastor Fliedner of Kaiserswerth (see later) had offered her the position of superintendent of the Bethanien hospital in Berlin, which she nonetheless declined.

17. Wednesday
Left Berlin   7½ A.M.
Hamburg   3½ P.M.
    Hotel de l'Europe very dear. Found Mlle Sieveking out. Went to her Infant Hospital, more lodging houses — & to Rauhe Haus.[124] Most interesting. I class you Geistliche Gebrüder [i.e.

---

122. Mary Keele (ed.), *Florence Nightingale in Rome*, p. 179.
123. *Life of Amelia Wilhemina Sieveking*, edited by Catherine Winkworth (London: Longman et al., 1863).
124. Rauhe Haus ("Ragged House") was an institution for the care of destitute boys founded by Johann Hinrich Wichern (1808–81), an evangelical theologian in Hamburg-Horn in 1833.

spiritual brothers] & Ragamuffins. Well satisfied with our lark —
& Richard was himself again.

Richard Monckton Milnes (1809–85) was a poet and a Member of
Parliament who had proposed marriage to Nightingale on several
occasions, but was finally declined sometime before she embarked
for Egypt. Her decision was not easily made as she confessed to
loving him, but she was compelled to refuse his proposal of marriage as she felt marriage would not provide her with the purposeful
life she longed to have:

> I have an intellectual nature which requires satis-
> faction and that would not find it in him. I have a pas-
> sionate nature which requires satisfaction and that would
> find it in him. I have a moral, an active, nature which
> requires satisfaction and that would not find it in his
> life. . . .
> I know that if I were to see him again, the very
> thought of doing so quite overcomes me. I know that,
> since I refused him, not one day has passed without
> my thinking of him, that life is desolate to me to the
> last degree without his sympathy. And yet do I wish
> to marry him? I know that I could not bear his life —
> that to be nailed to a continuation & exaggeration of
> my present life, without hope of another would be in-
> tolerable to me — that voluntarily to put it out of my
> power ever to be able to seize the chance of forming
> for myself a true & rich life would seem to me like
> suicide.[125]

Milnes was traveling en route to Marienbad when he met up with
Nightingale in Hamburg. A year after seeing her in Germany, he
married Annabel Crewe. Although his proposal to Nightingale had
been refused, Milnes nevertheless remained her lifelong friend and
ardent supporter. In his poem "A Moment for Scutari" (1855) he
devoted a stanza to her work.

---

125. BM Add. MSS 43402.f 53–54.

Much has been made of Nightingale's decision not to marry even in light of her own explanations given here. In a 'psychohistorical' study, Donald Allen conjectured that as a result of conflicts with her mother, Nightingale exhibited "feminine masochism," citing Helene Deutch's 1944 book *The Psychology of Women.*[126] In such cases, Allen wrote, a woman may become "erotically isolated," her "attitude toward life may be very active and masculine," and she may undertake willingness to serve a cause or a human being with love and abnegation."[127] Nightingale's humanitarianism and compassion are thus viewed as masochistic, rather than altruistic. Such an interpretation completely trivializes the sincerity of her spiritual calling, which would become in Allen's hypothesis merely a neurotic symptom of a sexually immature woman.

As further evidence of her neurosis, Allen indicates that Nightingale was "ready to attach herself passionately to any other female." Likewise, F. B. Smith remarked that Nightingale's "sexual relationships remained infantile," and that "her emotional attachments were directed to her own sex and from adolescence onwards she engaged occasionally in sentimentally effusive protestations of love for various female relatives and acquaintances."[128] These authors, however, fail to see Nightingale's relationships with women within the context of Victorian culture, which not only permitted but *encouraged* romantic friendships between women (with little thought of sexuality by either observing men or perhaps even the women themselves).[129] Of necessity women turned to each other for intellectual, emotional, and spiritual support, as did men with each other, since associations with the opposite sex were strictly defined, especially among the upper classes. Thus, Nightingale's affectionate relationships with her closest female friends and relatives are not exceptional, however "effusive" they may seem from a twentieth-century perspective. Whether or not

---

126. Donald R. Allen, "Florence Nightingale: Toward a Psychohistorical Interpretation," *Journal of Interdisciplinary History*, 6:1 (Summer 1975), pp. 23–45.

127. Ibid., p. 32.

128. *Florence Nightingale: Reputation and Power* (New York: St. Martin's Press, 1982), pp. 21, 23.

129. Lillian Faderman, *Surpassing the Love of Men: Romantic Friendship and Love Between Women from the Renaissance to the Present* (New York: William Morrow, 1981), pp. 119 ff.

there was any sexual component to these relationships is impossible to establish with any certainty. Even devoid of sexuality, Faderman believes "there is little to distinquish romantic friendship from lesbianism,"[130] and thus Dell Richards included Nightingale among her *Superstars: Twelve Lesbians Who Changed the World*.[131] In a rare moment of insight, F. B. Smith perhaps most accurately stated: "Ultimately she had made a mystic marriage with God's work."[132]

18. Thursday
Called upon Mlle Sieveking at 7. She was quite willing to talk about her plans — her educating the sick, that they may think themselves bound to lead an useless life.

Hamburg   8 A.M.
Harburg   10½
Hannover   4½

  Took Lohnkutsche [i.e. a carriage] & off for Pyrmout before 6 P.M. which we reached at 3 A.M. Very pleasant quiet journey by moonlight through woods. Hannover as dull as ditch water.

19. Friday
Pyrmont.
Our lark having answered so well today we rested & wrote letters.

20. Saturday
Took a vapor bath, wrote letters & read *Shirley*.

Shirley is the title of a novel written by Charlotte Brontë published in 1849. There is much in this novel about the plight of women with which Nightingale would have identified. Set amid the labor

---

130. Ibid., p. 142.
131. New York: Carroll & Graf, 1993.
132. Smith, p. 23.

unrest in northern England in the early nineteenth century, the novel focuses on the lives of two very different women: Shirley Keeldar, the independent and vivacious heiress, and the demure and dutiful Caroline Helstone. While Shirley's wealth affords her more freedom than what her sex normally permits, Caroline is dependent upon her uncle for her livelihood as she has no immediate family nor income of her own. Desiring some form of activity to engage her mind, Caroline:

> would wish nature had made her a boy instead of a girl, that she might ask [her cousin] Robert to let her be his clerk, and sit with him in the counting-house, instead of sitting with Hortense in the parlour (ch. 6).

Similarly, Nightingale wrote in a private note intended for her parents: "You must look upon me as your son."[133] When Caroline's plans to marry Robert fall through, she becomes despondent with no hope of a purposeful life: "I often wonder what I came into this world for. I long to have something absorbing and compulsory to fill my head and hands, and to occupy my thoughts" (ch. 12). Despite her pleas for some meaningful occupation, her uncle is unsympathetic, exhorting her to "learn shirt-making and gown-making, and pie-crust-making" for these will make her a clever woman. Faced with an idle, stifling, and unfulfilling life as a devoted daughter, Nightingale would certainly have identified with Caroline's dilemma and sentiments. She would have seen clearly, if not painfully, her own plight in the following passage describing Caroline's ensuing depression:

> Life wastes fast in such vigils as Caroline had of late but too often kept; vigils during which the mind, — having no pleasant food to nourish it — no manna of hope — no hived-honey of joyous memories — tries to live on the meagre diet of wishes, and failing to derive thence either delight or support, and feeling itself ready to perish with craving want, turns to philosophy, to resolution, to resignation; calls on all these gods for aid, calls vainly, — is unheard, unhelped, and languishes (ch. 20).

---

133. Vicinus & Nergaard, p. 55.

Likewise, Nightingale might have been comforted by Brontë's admonition:

> Yet, let whoever grieves still cling fast to love and faith
> in God: God will never deceive, never finally desert him.
> 'Whom He loveth, He chasteneth.' These words are true,
> and should not be forgotten (ch. 20).

Like Nightingale, Brontë turned down several offers of marriage as she was reluctant to sacrifice her own personal fulfillment. With limited of means of support, she made several unsuccessful attempts as a teacher and governess, two of the few occupations open to women. In *Shirley*, she frequently used the character of Caroline to voice her frustrations with the lack of opportunties for women:

> I believe single women should have more to do — better
> chances of interesting and profitable occupation than
> they possess now. . . . The brothers of these girls are every
> one in business or in professions; they have something
> to do: their sisters have no earthly employment, but
> household work and sewing; no earthly pleasure. . . . This
> stagnant state of things makes them decline in health:
> they are never well; and their minds and views shrink
> to wondrous narrowness. The great wish — the sole aim
> of every one of them is to be married, but the majority
> will never marry: they will die as they now live. (ch. 22)

Later, in *Suggestions for Thought*, Nightingale would fire an attack on family life, calling it a prison from which men could escape but that relegated women to the roles of dutiful daughters or obedient wives:

> What are we to do with girls? It is vaguely taken for
> granted by women that it is to be their first object to
> please and obey their parents till they are married. But
> the times are totally changed since those patriarchal
> days. Man (and woman too) has a soul to unfold, a part
> to play in God's great world.[134]

---

134. *Suggestions for Thought* (Calabria & Macrae), p. 104.

Unknown to Nightingale, the author of *Shirley* led the very kind of existence against which Nightingale railed: she married late in life to secure her own livelihood as well as that of her eldery father for whom she cared. Less than a year after her marriage in 1854, Brontë died. Had these two women ever met, they certainly would have had much to discuss.

22. Monday
Poor little dove came.[135]

23. Tuesday
Pyrmont.
Sate under the trees of the garden with Elise talking philosophy.

28. Sunday
Went to the Lutheran Church.
Justus Adelberg came — a philosopher & a republican.[136]

31. Wednesday
Kaiserswerth.
At 5 A.M. set off on my travels with Elise & Trout. Reached Herford at 12. parted with Elise — dismissed the Lohnkutsche, & took the sail to Calcum, 6.30 P.M.
　　　Kaiserswerth 8. I could hardly believe I was there — with the feeling with which a pilgrim first looks on the Kedron,[137] I saw the Rhine — dearer to me than the Nile. The Fliedners received me kindly.

---

135. A pet name for a Miss Adelberg, a German governess, for whom Nightingale tried to secure employment in England and the United States. (See letters of April and May 1847, copies in the Wellcome Institute.)
　　136. Probably the brother of Miss Adelberg, the 'poor little dove' referred to above.
　　137. A brook that flows through a valley between Jerusalem and the Mount of Olives: ". . . Jesus went out with his disciples across the Kedron ravine. There was a garden there, and he and his disciples went into it." (John 18:1, Revised English Bible)

Due to the lack of Protestant religious orders, particularly for women, Protestant communities often lacked social welfare institutions such as hospitals and orphanages traditionally run by Catholic sisters. To fill this need, Evangelical pastor Theodore Fliedner (1800–64) and his wife established the Institution of Deaconesses (Diakonissen Anstalt) at Kaiserswerth near Düsseldorf. Originally founded in 1833 as a refuge for released female convicts, the institution was expanded to include a hospital, nursery school, orphanage, and school for women teachers. Women who wished to become deaconesses underwent a probationary period of up to three years. Once accepted as deaconesses they served a five-year period, after which time they could renew their commitment or leave the institution.[138] Religious education was an integral part of training for deaconesses, although no vows were made such as in Catholic orders. Deaconesses read Bible selections and sang hymns with patients in addition to caring for their physical needs.

At the time of Nightingale's visit, there were 116 deaconesses at Kaiserswerth. The hospital that contained 100 beds comprised four wards: the Men's ward (Männer Station), the Women's ward (Frauen Station), the Children's ward (Kinder Station) for girls under seventeen years and boys under six, and a ward for boys over six. Women trained as nurses at Kaiserswerth were in great demand, and were sent to serve at other hospitals or wherever the need arose. By 1864 Fliedner had helped found thirty similar institutions across Europe, in North America, and in the Middle East, attended to by 1,600 deaconesses.

Kaiserswerth was to be the pinnacle of Nightingale's journey abroad. For four years she had dreamed of going there ever since she first learned of the institution from Christian von Bunsen. In 1846, she had prophesied: "There is my home, there are my brothers and sisters all at work. There my heart is and there, I trust, will one day be my body."[139] She had hoped to visit Kaiserswerth in the fall of 1848 while her mother and sister took the cure at Carlsbad, but political unrest in Germany prevented them from traveling.

---

138. *Life of Pastor Fliedner of Kaiserswerth*, Catherine Winkworth, trans., (London: Longmans, Green, 1867).
139. Cook, vol. 1, p. 64.

There is little information on how Nightingale's stay at the Institution was arranged. When she returned there for a second stay in 1851, she wrote that her first trip had come about in such a way that she was not at liberty to tell.[140] The first mention of Kaiserswerth in her diary occurs in March soon after she "settled the question with God," perhaps an allusion to her decision to go to Kaiserswerth. Apparently her family was not to know of her plans. Her mother, in particular, had already made it clear that nursing was not an acceptable activity. Before leaving Greece Florence explained in a letter to her family that since her travel plans were still uncertain, letters should only be sent to her in Vienna, Dresden, and Berlin.[141] After she mailed her last letter to them from Trieste on June 25, they would not hear from her until she returned to England in August.

August

1. Thursday
Went over the Institution with Fliedner — returned with him to dinner. Sate the afternoon with her & the Russian in the garden. My hope was answered. I was admitted within the Diakonissen Anstalt. Went to the Inn to dismiss Trout & get my things. My first night in my own little room within the Anstalt. I felt queer, but the courage which falls into my shoes in a London drawing room rises on an occasion like this. I felt so sure it was God's work.

2. Friday
Up & breakfasted by 7 in my own little room. In the Kinder Station with Schwester [Sister] Katerina. Down to the Rhein bank with the children. Dined at 12 bei [at] Pastor's. He & his wife,[142] housekeeper, Deaconisse & Probepflegerinn [novice-nurse],

---

140. Sticker, Anna. *Florence Nightingale: Curriculum Vitae* (Dusseldorf-Kaiserswerth: Diakoniwerk, 1965), p. 7.

141. BM Add. MSS 45,790.f55.

142. After the death of his first wife in 1841, Fliedner married Caroline Bertheau who had been a student of Amalie Sieveking's and who had served as a superintendent at the Hamburg Infirmary.

Luise[143] & sister & brother, two clerks Candidut & Econom.
Drank coffee at 3 in my own room. Supped at 7 w/ Pastors.

3. Saturday
Kinder Station.
Anstalt's Prediger Stunde [sermon hour] to the children — 5 P.M.

4. Sunday
Kinder Station
With Schwester Caterina to Church (in the Anstalt) 9.30 A.M. After
dinner, her exposition to the children, looking at parallel prayers
in their bibles. After tea, her story first to the little ones, then to
the big ones, not a Bible story — then her Evening devotions &
extemporary prayer. Walked in garden with the Fliedners till dark.
    Sate up till 1.30 A.M. with the Apothecary Sister. Every
hour went round into every ward.[144] Then we went to bed — I in
Schwester Julie's room.

5. Monday
8 A.M. Men's devotions with Sister Reichardt,[145] who explained
Chap. extern. Frauen Station–Schwester Henriette[146] &
Schwester Gottlieb.
    Fliedners Stunde 8 P.M. on Heb XII, 1–16.

6. Tuesday
Frauen Station
Anstalt Predigers Stunde 8 P.M.

7. Wednesday
Frauen Station
Luise Fliedner came to me at night.

8. Thursday.
Männer Station

---

143. Fliedner's daughter.
144. Each nurse served in rotation as night supervisor and made rounds every
hour during her shift. Male nurses, however, attended to the men's and boy's wards
in the evening.
145. Sister Gertrude Reichardt was the first deaconess at Kaiserwerth.
146. Sister Henrietta Frickenhaus was head of the infant school.

The Diary

81

Bibel Stunde [Bible lesson] to the Probe pflegerinnen [novice nurses] in the Probe Saal [novice hall] — Ranke.[147]

9. Friday
Asil — Schwester Elene
Gathered beans in the garden — Sister expounded John III. Girls told stories or sang, while they shelled the beans.
    Stations Stunde — Fliedner
Anniversary Fete of Lehrerinnen [teachers'] Seminar.

10. Saturday
Admission of new orphan, a birthday of another at the Waisenhaus [orphanage].

12. Monday
Montags Stunde [Monday lesson].

13. Tuesday
Left Kaiserswerth feeling so brave as if nothing could ever vex me again & found my dear people at Düsseldorf.

14. Wednesday
Cologne.
Gräfrath with Σ to see De Leuw about the eyes. By rail to Vohwinkel — by bus to Gräfrath — Miss Zinsdale stood[?] our friend & got us in.
    Off to Cologne — or rather to Deutz[148] by sail. Crossed the river.
    Saw the Cathedral that night. I hope never to see it again. Bavarian windows worst than any kaleidoscope.

15. Thursday
They went to Bonn — & I staid at Cologne doing my thing for Fliedners.[149] In the afternoon, went to Waisenhaus & a church or two.

---

147. Ranke was the schoolmaster who came to Kaiserswerth in 1841 to train the pupil-teachers and teach the younger sisters.
148. Deutz, located across the Rhine from Cologne, remained an independent town until 1888 when it became part of Cologne.
149. Pastor Fliedner asked Nightingale to write something about the Institution of Deaconesses. This, she did, but stipulated in a letter to him (August 19, 1850):

16. Friday
Up before 5 doing my Fliedner thing. Embarked at 10 in rail.
Ghent 10 P.M. — Rain made rails slippery — cause of delay.

17. Saturday
They staid at Ghent actually for me to finish my M.S. Worked
all day. In the evening went to see those stupid idle
Beguines.[150]

18. Sunday
Went to the Cathedral & to the Deaf & Dumb Asylum at the
Soeurs de la Charité.[151]
       Worked on my M.S. from sunrise copying it out fair.
       Took a walk around the town.

19. Monday
Finished my M.S. — they read it, Mr. B. corrected it & sent it off.
Went to see the Sister of Charity give a lesson to the Deaf &
Dumb — future tense comes first — then present & past.
       Blowing such a gale, we got into the rail for Calais which
we reached by 9 P.M. Too much wind to cross.

20. Tuesday
Blowing a gale — slows crossing from Calais to Dover. Cleared
our things by 2 o'clock train. Reached London at 6 P.M. Settled
our account. Slept in my old bed at the Burlington [Hotel]. How
many revolutions of mind I have celebrated there — a week today
since I left Kaiserswerth.

"As I have undertaken this little exercise in obedience to your wishes, I must be
allowed to stipulate that my name may never be mentioned in connexion with it"
(copy, Wellcome Institute, London). In this way, her family would not learn of her
stay there. The pamphlet was published in London in 1851 as "The Institution of
Kaiserswerth on the Rhine for the Practical Training of Deaconesses under the Di-
rection of the Rev. Pastor Fliedner, embracing the support and care of a hospital,
infant and industrial schools, and a female penitentiary."
       150. The Beguines were members of quasi-monastic sisterhoods founded in the
Low Countries in the twelfth century. They were not bound by vows in the tradi-
tional sense, and were devoted primarily to philanthropic work including nursing.
The reason for Nightingale's criticisms of the Beguines is unknown.
       151. The order of the Sisters of Charity of Jesus and Mary was founded in 1803
by Peter Triest. The order is active in primary and secondary school education, as
well as caring for the blind, mute, and handicapped.

21. Wednesday
Up at 5. Saw Σ off. Off myself by 8.30 from Euston Sq. Amber
Gate at 2 & home by 3 — Surprised my dear people sitting in the
drawing room & not thinking of me, with the owl in my
pocket[152] — J.P. came directly after — Fowlers in the evening.

22. Thursday
Sate with Mama & Papa in the nursery.
    Rode with Papa & J.P.

23. Friday
Prof. Pillans came.[154]

[end of the diary]

---

152. While in Athens, Nightingale rescued an owl that had fallen from its nest
on the Parthenon. She named the owl 'Athena' and made it her pet. Athena per-
ished while Nightingale was serving in the Crimea. The owl was stuffed and still
resides in the house at Lea Hurst.
    153. Perhaps James Pillans (1778–1864), the Scottish educational reformer.

1. Florence Nightingale, carte-de-visite by H. Lenthall, 1854. (National Portrait Gallery)

2. Lea Hurst, the Nightingales' summer house in Derbyshire

87

3. Embley Park, the Nightingales' winter house in Hampshire

4. Christian von Bunsen (1791–1860), Prussian ambassador, Egyptologist and friend of Nightingale's

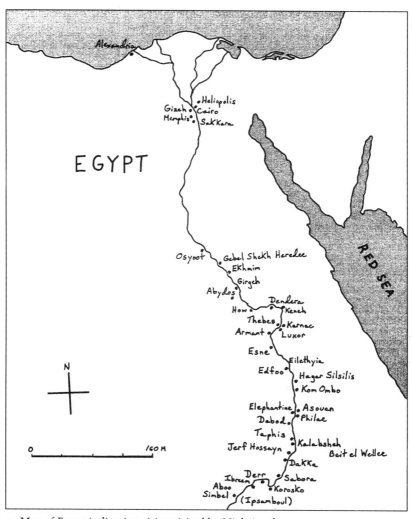

5. Map of Egypt indicating cities visited by Nightingale

90

6. "Thebes," a watercolor by Selina Bracebridge with a view of the Temple of Luxor (City of Birmingham Museum and Art Gallery)

7. The approach to Abu Simbel, Maxime Du Camp, c. 1850 (New York Public Library)

8. Colossi of Abu Simbel, Francis Frith, c. 1857 (New York Public Library)

93

9. The Temple of "Hermes Trismegistus" at Dakkeh, Maxime Du Camp, c. 1850 [New York Public Library]

94

10. "Approach to Philae," Francis Frith, c. 1857 [New York Public Library]

11. "Pharaoh's Bed, Island of Philae," Francis Frith, c. 1857 (New York Public Library)

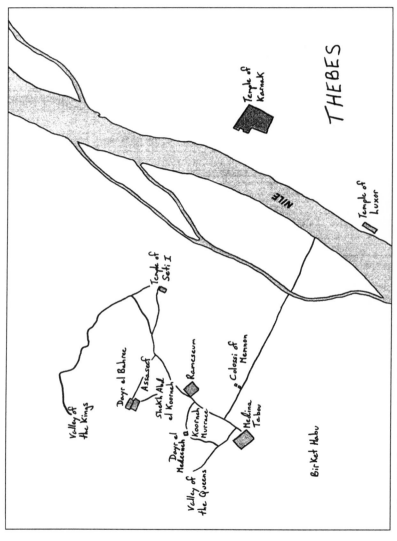

12. Map of Thebes indicating sites visited by Nightingale

13. "The Temple of El-Karnak," Francis Frith, c. 1857 (Scottish National Portrait Gallery)

98

14. "The Valley of the Tombs of the Kings," Francis Frith, c. 1857 (New York Public Library)

15. "The Rameseum of El-Kurneh," Francis Frith, c. 1857 (Scottish National Portrait Gallery)

16. "Interior of the Hall of Columns, Karnak," Francis Frith, c. 1857 (Scottish National Portrait Gallery)

17. The Temple of Sethos at Koorneh, Maxime Du Camp, c. 1850 [New York Public Library]

102

18. Step Pyramid of Djoser at Sakkara (author's collection)

103

19. "The Great Pyramid and the Sphinx," Francis Frith, c. 1857 (New York Public Library)

104

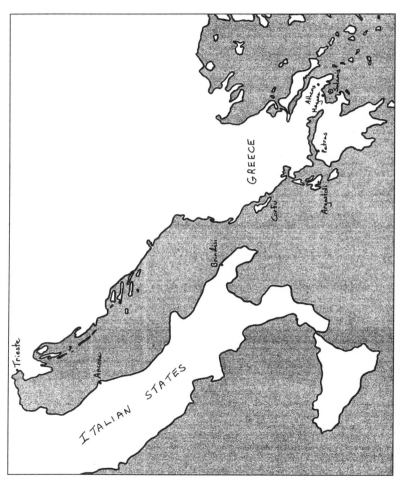

20. Map of Greece and Italy indicating places mentioned by Nightingale

105

21. The Acropolis, watercolor by Selina Bracebridge (City of Birmingham Museum and Art Gallery)

22. North side of the Acropolis, watercolor by Selina Bracebridge (City of Birmingham Museum and Art Gallery)

23. The Parthenon seen from the Propylaea (author's collection)

24. "The Temple of Jupiter Olympus, Athens," D. Constantin, c. 1860 (New York Public Library)

25. Map of Europe indicating cities visited by Nightingale

26. Raphael's "Sistine Madonna" (Dresden): "what woman might be, was intended to be."

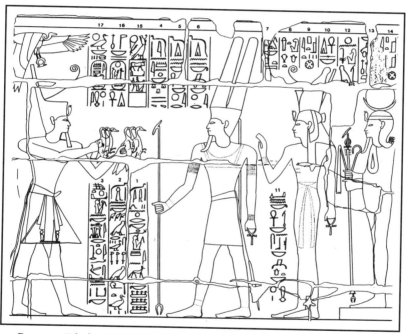

27. Rameses II before the Great Triad of Thebes: Amun, Mut, and Khonsu (from the Temple of Karnak). Source: H. Nelson and W. Murnane, *The Great Hypostyle Hall at Karnak* (University of Chicago, 1981)

28. Rameses II being led by the gods Atum and Montu (from the Temple of Karnak). Source: H. Nelson and W. Murnane, *The Great Hypostyle Hall at Karnak* (University of Chicago, 1981)

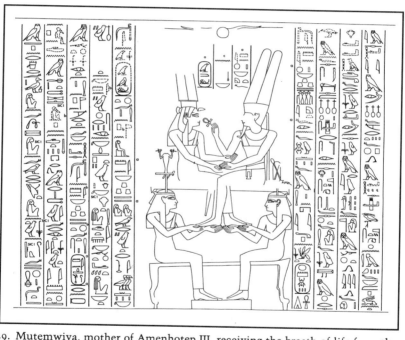

29. Mutemwiya, mother of Amenhotep III, receiving the breath of life from the god Amun-Re (from the Temple of Luxor). Source: Hellmut Brunner, *Die Geburt des Gottkönigs* (Harrasowitz, 1986)

30. Mutemwiya, mother of Amenhotep III, being led to the delivery chamber by the god Khnum and the goddess Hathor. (from the Temple of Luxor). Source: Hellmut Brunner, *Die Geburt des Gottkönigs* (Harrasowitz, 1986)

31. "a hall of columns like a forest of the West," Temple of Karnak (author's collection)

32. "And he lighted his temple with the light of heaven from above." Clerestory grate from the Temple of Karnak (author's collection)

33. Seti I being purified with the water of life by Seth and Horus (from the Temple of Karnak). Source: H. Nelson and W. Murnane, *The Great Hypostyle Hall at Karnak* (University of Chicago, 1981)

PART II

Vision of Temples

In the diary entry for July 9, 1850, Nightingale wrote that one of the paths that she might have chosen was a literary career. With their vivid and poetic descriptions of the ancient monuments and the Egyptian landscape, her letters from Egypt indicate that she did indeed have a gift for writing. This is further demonstrated by her fictional "Vision of Temples," which was appended to her letters in the 1854 edition. In its form, the "Vision" is a yarn in which Nightingale wove fact and fiction to explain the origin of several major Egyptian temples, namely, those of Deir el-Bahri, Luxor, Qurna, Karnak, the 'Rameseum,' and Medinet Habu, built principally during the eighteenth to twentieth dynasties (c. 1539–1075 B.C.). Judged by the subject matter and similarities in style to her letters, it would appear that Nightingale wrote the "Vision" during or not long after her visit to Thebes in February 1850. Although there is no mention of the "Vision" in the diary, Nightingale does refer to it in a letter to her family: "Keep my 6 churches of Thebes for me . . . if you have have it. I could have written that so much more truly, if I had had time. It vexes me to think how much more true I might have made it."[1]

Two major themes are presented in Nightingale's "Vision": (1) that humanity's concept of God is imperfect and (2) that humanity's comprehension of the divine nature increases through an evolution of consciousness. Both ideas were later explored at length in *Suggestions for Thought*, a draft of which she completed within two years after her return from Egypt. In the complete work, privately printed in 1860,[2] she rejected conventional views of a capricious God and beliefs such as the atonement, incarnation, and eternal damnation. Instead, she presented her concept of a benevolent God whose creation functions according to universal laws. These laws were the means by which mankind, the "Son of God," underwent an evolution of consciousness and thus became one *with* God. With its regular climate and the annual inundation of the Nile, Egypt presented a unique opportunity for

---

1. Letter of April 24, 1850 (BM Add. MSS 45790.f.13).
2. Some evidence suggests that Nightingale actually began writing the book in the 1840s. Only a few copies of the final work were printed for examination by friends and colleagues. *Suggestions for Thought: Selections and Commentaries* (Calabria and Macrae, eds., 1994). C.f. Mary Poovey's *Cassandra and Suggestions for Thought* (New York University Press, 1992).

Nightingale to observe God's laws that could then explain, and consequently eliminate, social ills. She wrote:

> God seems to have created Egypt as the personfication of law—a country without rain, without variations of climate—its food annually provided for it by an annual phenomenon, without example in the world for its regularity, beginning and ending on a certain fixed day. It makes the character of an Egyptian so different from that of the self-dependent, liberty-seeking European, that it seems as if Egypt was the very land for the observation of cause and effect; so much more certain must the noting down of consequences be here. Disease, weather, *returns* of every kind, from the public health to the causes of crime, might be here so much more easily calculated than anywhere else, that the things which seem to us *most* variable, most precarious, and *least* fit to find a place in any almanac we can construct, may in Egypt be actually (by studying the law, which is easily discoverable) made the subjects of law.[3]

Many of the ideas that Nightingale later presented in *Suggestions for Thought* are already nascent in her letters from Egypt and the "Vision of Temples." It is thus reproduced here in its entirety, followed by a discussion of the ideas presented therein and how they relate to those developed at length in *Suggestions for Thought*. The "Vision" begins with an introduction for the benefit of her family, introducing them to the temples, the deities to whom they were dedicated, and the kings who built them.

My dearest, the enclosed will give you no idea of the temples of Thebes, but it is what they said to me. Such as I have give I thee. To me the six temples of Thebes were the efforts of different characters, successful and unsuccessful, according to the state

---

3. *Letter from Egypt* (1854 ed.), p. 246. (This passage does not appear in Sattin's edition.)

of the vessel, as in the case with all inspiration, to render into form the inspirations of each member of the Great Triad of Thebes, Amun, Maut, and Khonso (fig. 27).[4]

Karnak   Amun, the
                        of
Medina Tabou   "Concealed" God,
          built by Sethos I. B.C. 1397;
          and Rameses III. B.C. 1290.

Luxor   Maut, Nature,
                        of
Koorna   Mother of all things,
          built by Amunoph III. B.C. 1478;
          and Rameses I. B.C. 1409.

Dayr-el-Bahree   Khonso—Strength or grace;
                        of
          Horus—Eros, or the world,
              or beauty, or order;
The Rameseum   Thoth—Wisdom;
                        these were all the same,
          built by Thothmes III. B.C. 1557;
          and Rameses II. B.C. 1388.

Rameses II. seems to have had a peculiar affection for Atmoo,[5] a Theban form of his own Ra,[6] whose name means to "complete" or "perfect;" and his whole temple bears the impress of his love of harmony. Atmoo leads him into the presence of the god (fig. 28)— Atmoo writes his name, &c. Rameses III, on the contrary, reminds me perpetually of Solomon, whose book Ecclesiastes he might have written, I think.

---

4. Usually rendered as: Amun, Mut, and Khonsu. Amun, was the god exemplar of the Egyptian empire. He was worshipped in the great temples of Karnak and Luxor along with his wife, Mut (whose name means "mother") and their son, Khonsu, associated with the moon.
    5. Now usually rendered as Atum.
    6. The sun-god. Atum and Re are sometimes combined as Atum-Re.

VISION OF TEMPLES

And the sons of the Theban kings presented themselves before the Lord. And He said, Behold, I send you upon the earth to govern, and raise the nation that I love. Build me a house that I may dwell in. And the sons of the kings said, What house, Lord?

And the spirit of the third Thothmes descended upon earth. And he said, Behold, God has sent me to drive out the invader from the land, and to glorify his name in the nation that he loves, that there may be none like her upon the earth. So he went forth with the bow and with the sword, and the enemy fled before him, with their hosts 240,000 men; and he pursued with his chariots and his horses till the land was utterly purged from their feet; and the glory of the kingdom of Egypt was great; there was none like her in all the world.[7]

Then the soul of the third Thothmes exulted within him, and he said, I have raised the glory of the God of hosts, the Lord of Strength shall be his name; and I will choose me out a high place which shall overlook all the land; on the high places of the earth shall be the dwelling of my God; whence He shall see the beautiful land of Thebes, whose glory is above the kingdoms of the world. And he chose him the heights of Dayr-el-Bahree.[8] And he built there a temple for the God of armies; for he said, Glory and Strength are my God. By the strength of my arm and the power of my intellect, have I gotten myself the victory.

And he offered to God all his riches, and all his mighty spoils, and me made a list, and he inscribed it with the names and the numbers of the vessels of silver and vessels of gold which he had given to the Lord. And he said, Surely His glory is great, and mine also.

---

7. According to the state of Egyptological knowledge in Nightingale's day, Thuthmosis (or Thothmes) III had driven the Asiatic invaders known as the Hyksos out of Egypt. It has since been determined that the Hyksos were driven out by Ahmose I (c. 1539–14 B.C.).

8. Although Thuthmosis III did build a small temple at Deir el-Bahri, the temple to which Nightingale is referring was actually that of the female pharaoh Hatshepsut (c. 1475–58 B.C.), called "Mephra" in Nightingale's letters. Sometime after her death, Thuthmosis III expunged Hatshepsut's name from her monuments and claimed them for himself. Later, German Egyptologist Richard Lepsisus concluded that Thuthmosis III had actually claimed Hatshepsut's temple as his own. Although significant excavation on the temple did not occur until 1858, enough of the temple was visible in Nightingale's day to draw tourists to the area.

And he reigned forty years, and his spirit returned to God who gave it.

And it came to pass that, after four and thirty centuries, the spirit of Thothmes returned to the land of his forefathers. And he revisited the Dayr-el-Bahree, and behold! not one stone remained upon another. And he said, How is this, Lord? And the Lord said, Because thou didst think that I loved glory, and that my greatness was in my strength, and in much show that I took pleasure, and didst love thy own glory therewith a little; therefore have I thrown down thy edifice, so that one stone does not stand upon another. And didst thou think that the Lord, who hideth himself, whose mighty works go their still and silent course, without wakening one little bird that sleeps under its mother's wing; who has given his children to perform more beautiful works than he has done himself, and who suffers them to think them their own; who has given to them to create with toil and trouble, that they might have the satisfaction of thinking, "I have done this,"—didst thou really think that He had for his object his own glory, and that his servants were to seek first, not the "*kingdom* of God," but his regalia and his coronation clothes?

And the spirit of the third Amunoph was sent upon earth. And he overran all the land as far as Mesopotamia, and he called himself the Lord of Truth;[9] and he said, I am become like unto God.

Therefore, he said, I will build a temple to nature, for by the laws of the universe have I conquered, and she is my mother. And he chose out a place by the river side, fertile and full of corn and cattle, and he called it El-Uksur [i.e. Luxor]; because, he said, I have built me palaces for the mother of all things. And he remembered his own mother, who nursed him upon her knee so tenderly, and who governed the kingdom so wisely during his wars; and to her he dedicated chambers in his temple,[10] and he made many dark places and secret chambers, and a holy place into which no eye

---

9. Refers to Amenhotep III's *prenomen*, or 'throne name,' *Neb-ma'at-Re*, which may be translated as "Lord of the Truth of Re."

10. This refers to the rooms that contain reliefs detailing the king's "divine birth." According to the account, Amenhotep is the offspring of the god Amun

could see; because, he said, Night is the genesis of all things; primeval darkness is the mother of the world, for darkness is more ancient than light, and day was born of night.

So rested he in "Nature, not the God of Nature," and forgot that darkness is good only, because out of darkness proceedeth light.

And after three and thirty centuries of purification, the spirit of Amunoph revisted the temple he had made, and he found it full of unclean beasts and creeping things; and of the unclean things, of all the dogs, and goats, and asses, the most unclean was man; and vilest of the creeping things and most abject was man.

And Amunoph said, My kingdom has become a base kingdom, and my temple the dwelling of beasts, not of gods, nor even of men.

And God said, Because thou hast worshipped Nature, not me; because thou hast seen law, not the God of laws, in the world around thee; because thou didst think thou couldst become the Lord of Truth by observing truth, therefore have I filled thy temple with that thou didst seek: lo! there is nature and natural life crawling about thy ruins.

Thou must be the servant of Truth, not her Lord, and Truth must be thy master.

But because thou hast loved thy mother, and preferred her in honour; because it was not thy own glory thou didst seek, therefore have I not destroyed thy temple—it shall stand, but stand as a den of beasts.

And God said, I will send a new race[11] upon the earth to govern Thebes, my chosen. And he sent the spirit of the first of the Rameses.

And Rameses said, I will build a temple for the great God. Yet, said he, not so, for how can the Unknown be known? how can the *Spirit* find a *place*? how can the Concealed be manifested? I

who impregnated Amenhotep's mother, Mutemwiya (figs. 29 and 30). The same fiction had been utilized previously by Hatshepsut and is recorded at Deir el-Bahri.

11. The Ramessides who ruled in the nineteenth dynasty were from the eastern Delta and thus of a different racial mix than the southern Theban kings of the eighteenth dynasty.

will seek me out a place under the shadow of the palms in the cool of the garden; and it shall be dedicated not to the glory of God, but to the manifestation of God—to Nature, the benevolent mother. And at Koorna, where the palm trees grew the tallest, where the mimosas were the greenest, and the shades were the freshest; where the sound of the sakia was heard, and the women brought their flock to water, there he built the house to the manifestation of his God; but pure was the spirit and bright the soul of the builder, and short was his purification; for before the temple was finished, his spirit had been recalled to the God who gave it. No monument records his wars; nor are his name or his glories found on the stela, nor in the tomb;[12] but morning and evening the Theban maiden came with her flocks and herds to sit upon the steps of his colonnade, and to look out over the fields of waving corn, and under the shade of the groves to the eastern palaces, and the distant hills, and bless his peaceful name.

And when Rameses revisted the earth, not to dwell there, but to see his children and his children's children making his name eternal, he found his temple completed in his name; he found justice done here in his name in the great hall of the temple set apart for it; he found religious assemblies, and political, the incarnation of the religious, here held; he found his son loving his memory, and his son's son loving *his* father's, and binding up their names in one.

And there, though the voice of the speaker and the tongue of the preacher have long been dumb, the flocks and herds still come, the acacias are ever green, and the sun still sets upon the amethyst crown of Thebes.[13]

And the spirit of the first Sethos was sent upon the earth— the warrior, the artist, the philosopher, the tender and conscientious heart.

---

12. Few monuments of Rameses I have survived from his brief two-year reign. Nightingale visited his tomb in the Valley of the Kings (see diary entry for February 19).

13. A reference to the mountains in western Thebes, which take on a purplish hue as the sun sets.

Shall I build a house unto the Lord? he said. I will, but it shall be a house to the great Unknown, the Unutterable, the Infinite Himself; to Him to whom great things are as small, and small things as great; to Him to whom a thousand years are but as a day, and a day as a thousand years; to Him who creates good and evil, who has formed darkness as well as light.

I will build a temple, he said, mysterious as the future, and vast as the past; yet it shall be the symbol of a day—of so small and definite a thing as a day, that my people may know that upon the hours of a day are laid the destinies of man. Karnak itself shall be but the image of a day.

And he built a temple to the one God, such as the world had not seen, a hall of columns like a forest of the West[14] (fig. 31); and the columns seemed to support the sky. Peradventure among them the Unseen will appear, he said. And there were six mighty columns on either side; for twelve are the hours of the day, and they are the pillars of man's soul, he said. Can we make the hours too great or too awful? for upon them is built the temple of man's perfection.

And on either side were raised sixty lesser columns, yet loftier and greater than any the eye of man had yet seen—the columns of the sixty minutes; for he said, The minutes makes the hours, that my people may not despise the "day of small things." So, when the shadow of those mighty columns moves round with the sun, shall my people see that every minute casts a mighty shadow upon the future, though it be but a little thing, even upon *all* the future. Each minute is great as our father time, for time hangs upon a minute.

And my temple shall be so high that it shall seem to connect earth and heaven; even so doth time, mysterious time, whose minutes flow on noiselessly like the sand, yet remain firm as the rock in their effect.

And he lighted his temple with the light of heaven from above, even as time, he said, is lighted by eternity[15] (fig. 32); and till the

---

14. Refers to the great hypostyle hall at Karnak. This vast hall measures 338 feet wide and 170 feet long and contains 134 columns. It is large enough in area to contain almost the entire Cathedral of Notre Dame.

15. Refers to the clerestory lighting that allowed light to penetrate the nave of the hall. The same device was later used in Romanesque and Gothic cathedrals in Europe.

light of eternity is thrown upon them, we cannot truly judge of our deeds.

And he said, Shall we have nought that is evil, have nought but the enervating good? Nay, but even with God impossibilities are impossible. Can man have the good of patience without suffering? have the good of happiness and the good of suffering, and both from happiness? Can he be taught without evil? the law he is to learn without enduring the consequence it has caused? But without consequences there would be no law.

Let us have evil, he cried, O my God.

And he caused himself to be represented gifted with life by the two spirits of God, Good and Evil, that all the people might see that their king accepted suffering (fig. 33).

And he called the Unknown God "Come;" because, he said, He "cometh" to his creatures and manifests himself unto them. And he said,

Nature is good, for she maketh him known. But Nature is not God; yet shall she lead me into the presence of God. And she did so.

And among the columns of his temple he found his God.

And he overthrew nothing which his fathers had raised, he carefully preserved it all; for he said, The Unknown is the God of my fathers also; they sought him after their manner, and we will all seek him, each after our own. But in the faithful observance of each daily hour and its occupation we shall find him best.

And he caused himself to be represented on his tomb with the chain of the hours round his neck, not heavily weighing him down, for each hour bears its own portion of the chain, its own burden, but binding him to *full-fill* his hour; for he said,

I am not the lord of my hours, but I am their servant; for each hour is a genius, a messenger of the unknown God. So I will seek my Lord, and then in the temple he shall "come" unto me.

Thus the vast mysterious temple of the immeasurable Karnac, and the stedfast procession of the little hours, alike witness of God to the mind of the true artist.

And when Sethos died, there was joy in heaven, and the spirits of heaven arose and went forth to meet him.

And he said, *"Come,"* Lord; and the Lord said, Here, my child.

And God said, His temple shall stand for ever, and that image of Good and Evil shall not be effaced; for my servant has read me aright, and the Unintelligible has become intelligible to him.

And Sethos returned from heaven to his own temple of Karnac, and he saw his own name forgotten, so that one man read it one way and one man another;[16] but his idea was still living. Of all the temple in the land of Thebes his alone showed forth to the world, clear as on the day which first saw them sculptured, the thoughts which had inspired him, and which shall still inspire man. And he said, It is well, Lord.

And he saw a silent and a melancholy northern race arise, and they visited his own loved land of the South, and they said,

We have suffered much Evil, yet a thought *comforts* us—it will pass away; this is but a world of trial, therefore we can endure.

And he said, I have suffered much Evil, but a thought *inspires* me—it will not pass away, it bestoweth life; this world is eternal, and giveth eternal life, therefore we need no *comfort*, for evil is but another name for good.

And the spirit of the great Rameses was sent upon earth, purified by intercourse with his father, he came—the warrior and the devout philosopher; and he delivered his nation from her enemies, and he said, It is the Lord.

And he said, We know the Lord but by his works—the Great First cause by its effects alone. Now, the first of its effects is harmony, therefore will I build a temple unto Harmony, unto Eros; for wherever the Lord is, there is Harmony, which is grace or strength.

And my temple shall have in it the sanctuary for the Intellect, and the sanctuary for Religion, and the sanctuary for Justice, and the sanctuary for Nature; for the Lord's grace is in all his works: ethically, it is Concord, the harmony of the Intellect and the Will; physically, it is Beauty or Order, the harmony of the active Intel-

---

16. When written plainly, Seti's name incorporates the hieroglyphic figure of the god Seth, the murderer of his brother Osiris and thus a god with evil connotations. Rather than evoking Seth by means of his image, in many instances the Set-hieroglyph in Seti's name is replaced with a hieroglyph representing Osiris—hence the confusion in reading the name.

ligence and Matter; morally, it is Eros or Love, the harmony of Intellect and Feeling; intellectually, it is Reason or Heavenly Science, the harmony of Power and Light. These are but forms of the
same, and in my temple there shall be a place for all.

And he built him a library for the learned, and a temple for
the devout, and a hall of justice for the people, and a tower to survey the world above and the world below, by night and by day; for
he said, All the faculties of man must be cultivated in harmony.

And he said, The Complete, the Perfect, shall be the Genius
of my temple, and the spirit of my mind; because Perfection, or
the harmony of all things, is the characteristic of God, who doeth
no exaggerated nor imperfect thing. My temple shall not be awful
in size nor stupendous in art, but it shall be finished in all its parts.

And he placed in the library the sacred books, and in the Hall
of Justice he placed statues of Thirty Judges, without hands, and
with eyes cast down, and an image of truth about their necks; because, he said, The judge should receive nothing, neither guided
by affection in his judgements, but his eyes should be intent on
Truth alone.

And he caused himself to be represented as conducted by the
spirit of "Completion" into the presence of God.

And he said, My temple shall not take up space in which man
can cultivate the fruits of the earth. Not so is the Lord's will; that
would be destroying the harmony which he has created. I will build
him an house on the edge of the desert, before the tombs, so shall
it join the two regions of life and death; and the winds of heaven
shall blow around it, and it shall stand upon a hill, so it cannot be
hid.

And he represented with himself his wife, and his daughter,
and his mother; because, he said, that we may be together in the
temple of the Lord.

And he said, "It is accomplished."

And in two and thirty centuries he returned upon the earth,
and the Lord was pleased with his temple, and with his servant's
offering: and he said, Thy temple shall stand, my son, and thy rec-
ollection shall not be effaced. Though thy own statue shall be over-
thrown, and the features thereof be disfigured and destroyed, yet
shall the devotion with which thou hast worshipped the Perfect
Goodness remain, and its influence shall not be wiped away from
the earth.

And the loving Nofriari[17] and her hero are still seen there side by side, worshipping the Perfect.

And there was an interval in Egypt: her power declined, her kingdom was given to strangers, her people to anarchy; her arts of peace and of war were forgotten; disorder reigned where once was concord.[18]

Then the third Rameses came upon earth, and he restored power to Egypt, and he extended the terror of his arm over all the earth, father even than his great forefathers had done. And he said: —

The earth is mine and the fulness thereof. Now will we dedicate ourselves to her pleasure and her glories, and whatsoever our eyes desire will we not keep from them. But the people believe in a God, in a [god] higher than me; therefore, as Ruler in the name of the Most High, shall I have more glory in their eyes. Therefore will I consecrate my coronation on the walls of a temple to the greatest of the gods, for He only is worthy to be my guardian deity, I will emblazon my victories on its stones, and they shall bear the record of the splendour of my power and the greatness of my name. And we will eat and drink and withhold not our hearts from any joy in the precincts of the Holy Place; and I will tread upon the necks of the "red-bristled barbarians," and I will say that He has put them under my feet.

And all that he said, even so he did; and sons and daughters were born unto him, and he said, I have established my kingdom for ever.

But from that hour there was no more prosperity in Egypt (though, when the stranger saw her luxurious he called her prosperous), and the sceptre passed away from the hands of Thebes; and of all the sons of Rameses, there was none to support the glory of his name. And religion, from being inspired, became laboured,

---

17. Rameses' "Chief Royal Wife." Her name is more often rendered as Nefertari.

18. Having outlived many of his sons, Rameses II was succeeded by his thirteenth son Merneptah. A struggle for the throne ensued upon Merneptah's death. After a series of short reigns, the twentieth dynasty commences with Setnakhte, father of Rameses III.

and that which was artificial was called art, and pomp was called power, till the throne was transferred to another land, and there were no more Rameses.[19]

And the third Rameses has not yet returned upon earth, though one and thirty centuries have been fulfilled, for he is wandering in weary ways: he must purify himself from the lust of the flesh in the form of a swine, from the lust of the eyes in the form of a peacock, and from the pride of life in the form of a stag; through forms of the lowest animals must he pass—a loathsome pilgrimage;[20] and when at last he revisits Thebes (not his beloved Thebes, except as ministering to his glory) he will find his temple hewn in pieces to serve another religion:[21] not a trace of his sacred place remaining, nought but the record of his pride and the memorial of his low ambition.

In 'Vision of Temples,' Nightingale utilizes the historical figures of Egyptian kings to illustrate the evolution in the concept of God, from that of a God of Power to an ineffable God embodying Perfection, Harmony, and Order. Her comments are *not* based on fact, but rather on impressions she gleaned from the monuments erected by the ancient kings. She begins with Thothmes (or Thuthmosis) III (1458–25 B.C.), the warrior-king of the eighteenth dynasty. For purposes of her story, Nightingale posited that his concept of God was imperfect as he believed God to be Power, the military might that granted him victory on the battlefield. Thus, he raised a temple to God's glory and his own. In *Suggestions for*

---

19. Rameses XI (1098–69 B.C.) was the last of the Ramessides. Following his death, Egypt ceased to be a united kingdom.

20. C.f., *Letters from Egypt* (February 10, 1850): "In the tomb of Rameses V (the second one we went into) we met one who had *not* been able to choose; he was revisiting earth in the form of a pig, having lived a sensual life, and extinquished within himself the spark of eternal life. At one end of the wall he was slowly mounting into the presence of Osiris; next, standing before him, himself weighing his *own* deeds, and then being 'found wanting,' he was leaving the divine presence, in the form of a wretched pig, driven by two monkeys. There was nothing ridiculous in this representation of the natural effect of sensuality; you could not laugh—you felt it as the inevitable necessity. If a man has allowed all that is divine (or human) within him to die out, how can it be other wise? Poor pig!"

21. In the early Christian era, a church occupied the second court of the temple.

Thought, Nightingale indicated that such erroneous concepts of God continue in the present as in the past:

> In these earlier nations, *power* seems to have been the principal characteristic of a God. He or she was merely an engine to account for creation. Take all the thousand different meanings, which have been attached to the word "God" by different nations and individuals in different ages, and some kind and degree of power above human seems to be all that is common to them. In these days we profess that we believe our God to be perfect, but we attribute to him all kinds of qualities that are not—love of His own glory, anger, indecision, change of mind—and we try to believe, if we think at all, that a God with these qualities is perfect.[22]

She indicated that as the word "God" has been used in various and vague ways over the centuries, "It would be the greatest gain religion has ever made, if, for a time, the word *God* . . . could be dropped, —and the conception substituted of a perfect being, the Spirit of Right."[23] Humanity comes to know God, the 'Spirit of Right,' and His will through His laws, which are constant and unchanging. She thus took issue with the positivism of Auguste Comte, whose philosophy was popular among intellectuals in the nineteenth century (Harriet Martineau, George Lewes, and George Eliot among them), since it reduced all existence to laws without a superior will behind them. In her view laws were nothing more than the thoughts of God. Although these laws are observable in nature, God cannot be equated with nature any more than an artist can be equated with his or her work of art. "Both pantheism and 'positivism' have a truth," she wrote, "but they leave us still without the all-comprehending thought, sentiment, appreciation, purpose, will. Comte sees law manifested throughout the phenomena of the universe, and sees nothing more."[24]

Thus, in the 'Vision,' Amunoph's (Amenhoptep III's) concept of God is also flawed for he declared God to be Nature (= panthe-

---

22. *Suggestions for Thought* (Calabria & Macrae), p. 18.
23. Ibid., p. 16.
24. Ibid., p. 40.

ism) and Law (= positivism), rather than seeing Nature and Law to
be expressions of God. His ideas are, however, an advance over
those of Thothmes' because he recognized the immanence of God,
and sought not to commemorate his own glory. Nightingale added
an element of hermetism to Amunoph's philosophy as evident
from the passage:

> Night is the genesis of all things; primeval darkness is
> the mother of the world, for the darkness is more an-
> cient than light, and day was born of night.

The idea of light arising out of darkness is a concept familiar to
Nightingale from the hermetic text *Pimander*, which she quoted
at length in a letter to her family (see earlier, p. 28f). For his increased, albeit incomplete, knowledge of God's character, Amunoph
undergoes 3,300 years of purification—100 years less than Thothmes.

With Rameses I, Sethos I, and Rameses II of Dynasty 19,
Nightingale found more enlightened concepts of God. Rameses I
recognized that God is Unknown and dedicated a temple not to
the glory of God, nor to Nature as God, but rather to Nature as the
manifestation of God. Similarly, Sethos I's God is 'the great Unknown, the Unutterable, Infinite Himself.' Like his predecessor,
he realized that nature cannot be equated with God but can lead
one into God's presence. Sethos goes still further, however, introducing a new concept of God: God who encompasses both good
and evil, light and darkness. This is perhaps the most radical element in Nightingale's theology, that evil is part of the Divine plan
because it alerts mankind to his errors and impels him to greater
good:

> What is the origin of evil? the question so often asked.
> The wisdom, goodness, and righteousness of the Perfect,
> the Father, is the answer; who wills that Man, the son,
> by the exercise of his nature in accordance with the laws
> of right, shall rise from ignorance to truth, from the im-
> perfect to the perfect.[25]

---

25. Ibid., p. 81.

It was a clever stroke on Nightingale's part to attribute this philo-sophical advance to Sethos as his name is actually that of the di-abolical god Seth who, according to myth, murdered his benevo-lent brother Osiris.

To Sethos' son, Rameses II, God is known by his works. He thus builds a temple to Harmony and Eros with sanctuaries to In-tellect, Religion, Justice, and Nature. A library, temple, and a hall of justice would serve as places where man could cultivate all his faculties in order to grasp God's true nature, which was Perfection itself. Likewise, in *Suggestions for Thought*, Nightingale wrote:

> It is evident that every nation, every age, *could* not be-lieve in a Perfect Being—that it required cultivation, de-velopment to conceive the idea of perfection, and that the higher all the faculties of an individual, as also of a nation, have been, the higher has been his conception of God, the nearer perfection.[26]

For his wisdom, Rameses' temple endured and he was purified after 3,200 years—100 years less than Amunoph (no years are given for Sethos' return). Contrary to his enlightened predecessors, Rame-ses III is concerned with his own glory and victory, and Egypt con-sequently experiences a decline. If his knowledge of God had pro-gressed as before, he would have been purifed after a period of 3,100 years—100 years less than Rameses II. Instead he is reincarnated in animal form for his transgressions and wanders still.

A prominent motif in the "Vision" is reincarnation, whereby the kings return and look upon their monuments. Nightingale was familiar with this concept from number of sources, including Her-metic and Platonic philosophy. In *Pimander*, the fate of the body and soul after death is described:

> At the dissolution of your body, you first yield up the body itself to be changed, and the visible form you bore is no longer seen. And your vital spirit you yield up to the atmosphere so that it no longer works in you; and the bodily senses go back into their own sources, be-

---

26. Ibid., p. 20.

coming parts of the universe, and entering into fresh
combinations to do other work.[27]

Similarly, in *Suggestions for Thought* Nightingale wrote:

> Is it asked, what being will live after this life ceases?
> Every mode of being which admits of thought and feel-
> ing. . . . Each individual thinking, feeling being, by the
> law of the Perfect, works upward, directly or indirectly, —
> attains to the perfect thought and feeling which com-
> prehends all, which feels and wills all truth, — and *then
> again sets forth to work and live, and manifest, and re-
> alize fresh phases of being, guided by the law of the all-
> comprehensive spirit.*[28] [my emphasis]

As early as 1846, she implied belief in reincarnation in a letter to
her cousin Hilary Bonham Carter:

> . . . And as long as Evil has its reign in this world, I want
> no other heaven, I can desire no further benefits, than
> to be allowed *to return & return with renewed & bet-
> ter powers from the Fountain of power*, till the King-
> dom of God is really come here. [my emphasis]

She would have also encountered the concept of reincarnation from
her studies of Plato, specfically the *Phaedo* and "The Myth of Er"
in *The Republic*, Book X. She also believed the Egyptians to have
held this belief:

> Osiris (the Goodness of God) calls the purified into a
> higher vocation, and the *same* Goodness sends back the
> impure under a new form, till it can present itself be-
> fore him cleansed from very lower feeling.[29]

Harriet Martineau, also influenced by Plato, spoke of reincarnation in *Eastern Life*, which Nightingale was reading at this time:

---

27. Scott, *Hermetica*, p. 52.
28. *Suggestions for Thought*, p. 152.
29. *Letters from Egypt* (1854 ed.), pp.224–25.

The three thousand years of purgatory of many of these
Theban sleepers is now about expiring. If their faith was
a true one, and they are now returning to resume their
bodies, and begin a new cycle, in what state will they
find their sumptuous death-chambers, and their hun-
dred-gated metropolis.[30]

The belief in reincarnation was not uncommon among Victorian
literatti and was held by William Wordsworth, Samuel Coleridge,
Robert Browning, Alfred Tennyson, and Matthew Arnold, as well
as Nightingale's suitor Richard Monckton Milnes and her secretary the poet Arthur Hugh Clough.[31] In addition to her remarks in
Suggestions for Thought and the "Vision of Temples," Nightingale also alludes to such a belief in her so-called "Greek Vision."

---

30. *Eastern Life*, vol. 2, p. 9.
31. Joseph Head and S. L. Cranston, comps., *Reincarnation: an East-West Anthology* (Wheaton, Ill.: Theosophical Publishing House, 1968).

PART III

A Greek Vision

This final section comprises an allegorical vision, which Nightingale probably composed in Greece, found as it is among her letters and notes from this time.[1] Like her "Vision of Temples," it is indicative of her gift for creative writing. The form of this vision is not unlike the Hermetic *Pimander*, which Nightingale knew well (see earlier, p. 27f), in which the mysteries of the cosmos are revealed to Hermes Trismegistus in a vision. The use of gemstones in the 'Vision' to symbolize certain qualities is also suggestive of the alchemical Hermetica of the Renaissance.[2] In this mystic quest, Nightingale seeks the answer to that quintessential question: "What is the meaning of Life?" As already seen in her diary, she believed that suffering and struggle are necessary components of life. Here, as in the "Vision of Temples," passing through several stages of existence (i.e., reincarnation) may be necessary before the soul joins the Divine.

In its form and style, this vision is not unlike a passage from Charlotte Brontë's *Shirley*, which, as we have seen, Nightingale was reading at this time (see earlier, July 20). In that novel, we read an allegory that tells of the union of Genius, represented as an invisible presence, and Humanity, portrayed as a young maiden. In a remarkable passage, which could not have failed to impress Nightingale, Humanity ponders her fate:

> The girl sat, her body still, her soul astir; occupied, however, rather in feeling than in thinking, — in wishing, than hoping, — in imagining, than projecting. She felt the world, the sky, the night, boundlessly mighty. Of all things, herself seemed to herself the centre, — a small, forgotten atom of life, a spark of soul, emitted inadvertent from the great creative source, and now burning unmarked to waste in the heart of a black hollow. She asked, was she thus to burn out and perish, her living light doing no good, never seen, never needed, — a star in an else starless firmament, — which nor shepherd, nor wanderer, nor sage, nor priest, tracked as a guide, or read

1. BM Add. MSS 43402 f. 41–44.
2. Frances A. Yates, *Giordano Bruno and the Hermetic Tradition* (Chicago: University of Chicago Press, 1991), pp. 44 ff.

as a prophecy? Could this be, she demanded, when the flame of her intelligence burned so vivid; when her life beat so true, and real, and potent; when something within her stirred disquited, and restlessly asserted a God-given strength for which it insisted she should find exercise? [ch. 27]

When a voice from heaven calls to her, she answers: "Lord!, behold thine handmaid!"—the words with which Mary answered the angel Gabriel at the anunciation (Luke 1:38), and with which Nightingale concludes her 'Greek Vision.' Although it does not appear that Nightingale borrowed the line from Brontë since she had used it on several occasions over the years to describe her own plight, it is nevertheless remarkable that these two authors were inspired similarly by the Gospel passage.

I stood at the pass of Thermopylae. The storm had ceased, and a rainbow was spanning the whole vault of God's broad heaven. I looked closer, and behold, a shadowy spirit lay in the folds of the rainbow. And I said, Who art thou?

And he said, I am Human Life, seest thou not how I divide Infinity on either hand & yet am finite. Infinite is the expanse of God's universe on either side my bow.

So Human Life has an Eternity before & behind it. Light stops its endless stream for a moment on a drop of water, I come forth, & though but a drop, Eternity waits to see what I shall do.

The form of the Rainbow was melting away. Stay, I cried, tell me what is Life, answer me but this & let me die.

And he answered, I will cause all my forms to pass before thee, ask them.

And all the hues of the rainbow seemed to take shape & form— and I saw, clad in the three first, Childhood's etherial grace, yet lovely in the blue robes of happiness straight from heaven, the sky, its home—& the first had a pure amethyst on its brow, & the second a sapphire, & the third a turquoise—for the three stages differed but by a paler tint of precious stone, as their "heavenborn" bliss faded away.

Next came Youth, clad in verdant hope, with his emerald chaplet.

And golden Manhood, laden with his harvest of yellow & orange (ripe and still riper) corn. And last of all came Old Age, crowned with rubies, for he was ready to be the Seraphim, the Burning Ones, glowing with love made perfect in disinterestedness, which Age, kind indulgent Old Age, alone can give. So the Seven Spirits, the Sons of Time, came floating by, each clothed in his Hue of Light.

And I felt on my face & cried, O ye radiant ones, tell me what is life, is it radiant as ye are?

And the first three spirits answered & sang, Life is "no holiday" sport, that thou shouldest say, it amuseth me not. I find neither excitement nor variety in it, sufficient for my thirst of them.

And the Emerald Spirit answered, Life is no book, that thou shouldest say, I would gather instruction, scientific & intellectual from it, that my mind may eat & be satisfied.

And the Golden Spirits answered, Life is no school, for thee to be intent upon working up all its materials into thy own improvement. Thinkest thou His Kingdom come, meaneth thy salvation come?

And the Last Spirit answered, Life is no valley of tears, that thou shouldest go through it, as through a desert, which thou must traverse, bearing & waiting. Whilst in the world there is Evil, Life is none of these things.

What is Life then, I cried?

And all the colours seemed to form themselves again into one white ray, & their voices to become one like the voices of the wind, & so say: Life is a fight, a hard wrestling, a struggle with the Principle of Evil, hand to hand, foot to foot—not only in thyself, nor *only* in the world, but in thyself as one in the world (in the world, in world in thyself). The kingdom of God is coming, but like other kingdoms, it must be won by the sword. Christ our Leonidas, this world our Thermopylae,[3] we the brave swords which keep the pass between Heaven & Hell. And the chariots & horsemen of God are with us. We go forth, arrayed in the panoply of perfect love; it is not our own salvation but the kingdom of God we fight for, & we

---

3. In 480 B.C., the Spartans under the leadership of their king Leonidas attempted to halt the the Persian advance at Thermopylae. All 300 Spartans and Leonidas were killed.

must fight till our last moment, perhaps through many stages of existence, till the Spirit & bride say, it is won—The night is given thee to take breath, to pray, to drink deep at the fountain of Power, the day to use the strength which hath been given thee, to go forth to work with it until the evening. At eve thou shalt pray. In the morning thou shalt go forth to war. Often wilt thou be worsted, often beaten down upon thy knees—but the good soldier, though sore wounded, & half dead, though hosts against him be many & strong, yet turneth him not to fly—for he is aware of the horsemen of the Lord, which fight at his right hand. The kingdom of God is coming, he cries, my life for my country & my God. Fight on, brave heart, courageously—the salvation of thy country hangeth on thy sword. Yield not an inch, let fall not thy arm, till the kingdom is fought for, the kingdom is won. So fights he & so bleeds he,—and the chariots & horses of fire are with him—till he sinks asleep on the turf of the valley.

The rainbow had vanished, the sun was setting, & I kneeled before it & said: "Behold the handmaid of the Lord," give me to morrow my work to do—no, not my work, but thine,—"& I did in the morning as I was commanded."[4]

---

4. C.f. Luke 1:38 : "And Mary said, 'Behold, I am the handmaid of the Lord; let it be according to thy word.'" Nightingale had referred to herself as the "handmaiden of the Lord" in a letter to Hilary Bonham Carter in 1846 (see earlier, p. 4).

CONCLUSION

Although she had left Kaiserswerth 'feeling so brave' as if nothing could ever vex her again, Nightingale's domestic life continued to be unbearable upon returning home. Her sister Parthenope was suffering from a nervous condition exacerbated, if not caused by (as her family would have it), Florence's frequent absences from home. When they learned of her trip to Kaiserswerth she was greatly chastised. In a letter to Henry Manning she wrote:

> I was in disgrace with them for a twelvemonth for going to Kaiserswerth. My sister has never spoken the word to me since. . . . I think the persecution of the Emperor Domitian must be easy to bear, but there is a persecution from those we love . . . which grinds one's very heart out, especially if one is not quite sure one is right.[1]

Barely a month after returning from her nine-month tour of Egypt and Greece, she fled from home again, this time to visit her Aunt Mai, as she would periodically over the next couple of years whenever she needed respite. She prolonged her visit as long as possible, writing to her parents for extensions on her leave. In a letter to her father she indicated the danger of continuing an idle life: "I see the numbers of my kind who have gone mad for want of something to do."[2] The pain and frustration she felt as a young woman confined by family obligations and expectations is articulated with vehemence in her *Suggestions for Thought*, a draft of which she was preparing at this time. In the section entitled "Cassandra" she protested: "The family uses people, *not* for what they are, nor for what they are intended to be, but for what it wants them for—for its own uses."[3]

---

1. Letter of July 1852; Shane Leslie, "Forgotten Passages in the Life of Florence Nightingale," *The Dublin Review*, vol. 161, no. 323 (October 1917): 184.
2. BM Add. MSS. 45790.f.107.
3. *Suggestions for Thought* (Calabria & Macrae), p. 99.

When news came in October of the death of her cousin Henry Nicholson, she dutifully went to attend her grieving relatives—anything was preferable to going back home. By December, however, she was compelled to return to Lea Hurst, and at the end of 1850 she was in utter despair and sadly wrote:

> I have no desire now but to die. There is not a night that I do not lie down in my bed, wishing that I may leave it no more. Unconsciousness is all that I desire. I remain in bed as late as I can, for what have I to wake for? I am perishing for want of food. & what prospect have I of better? While I am in this position, I can expect nothing else. Therefore I spend my day in dreams of other situations which will afford me food. Alas! now I do little else. For many years, such is the principal of hope. I always trusted that "this day month" [sic] I should be free from it. God, Thou knowest the efforts I have made. Now I do not hope. I know. I know that I, my nature & my position remaining the same, same nature cannot generate but same thoughts. Dec 30, 1851, I shall be much more unable to resist these dreams, being so much the more enfeebled. Starvation does not lead a man to exertion—it only weakens him. Oh weary days. Oh evenings that seem never to end—for how many long years I have watched that drawing room clock & thought it never would reach the ten & for 20 or so more years to do this. It is not the misery, the unhappiness that I feel so insupportable, but I feel this habit, this disease gaining ground upon me—& no hope, no help. This is the sting of death.
>
> Why do I wish to leave this world? God knows I do not expect a heaven beyond—but that He will set me down in St. Gile's,[4] or at Kaiserswerth, there to find my worth & my salvation in my work, that, I think will be the way, if I could but die.[5]

---

4. The parish of St. Giles-in-the-Fields in Soho was notorious for its poverty and squalor.
5. Private note dated December 30, 1850 (BM Add. MSS 43402 f.34).

She continued in this vein until the summer of 1851, when, perhaps to avoid further confrontation, her parents granted permission for her to return to Kaiserswerth for a three-month stay while Parthenope took the cure at Carlsbad. Even with their consent, she begged for their support and understanding:

> Give me time—give me faith. Trust me. Help me, I feel within me that I could gladden your loving hearts which now I wound. Say to me 'follow the dictates of that Spirit within Thee.' Oh my beloved people, that spirit shall never lead me to say things unworthy of me who is yours in love—Give me your blessing.[6]

The drama of Nightingale's plight is heightened because she viewed her struggle in religious terms: God had called her into His service and she longed to answer, but her plans were continually frustrated by family expectations. Desperately she prayed for faith to follow the command of the Spirit that communicated God's will to her. At her wit's end, she corresponded at length with Henry Manning about the possibility of converting to Catholicism and entering an order:

> But you do know now, with all its faults, what a home the Catholic Church is. And yet what is she to you compared with what she would be to me? No one can tell, no man can tell what she is to women—their training, their discipline, their hope, their home—to women because they are left wholly uneducated by the Church of England, almost wholly uncared-for-while men are not.
> For what training is there compared to that of the Catholic nun?[7]

When Manning expressed caution and commented on the 'eclecticism' in her beliefs, she impatiently retorted:

---

6. BM Add. MSS. 45,790: f 142.
7. *Ever Yours, Florence Nightingale: Selected Letters*, edited by Martha Vicinus and Bea Nergaard, (Cambridge, Mass.: Harvard University Press, 1990), p. 59.

> The Eclectic has been at least as strong an element as
> any other in filling the stream towards Catholicism.
> Why cannot I join it? . . . You will not perhaps believe
> it, but the search after Truth has been to me a martyr-
> dom, tearing up everything I love, forcing me upon con-
> clusions I recoil from, shutting the door upon what looks
> to me Paradise.[8]

Despite her urgent desire to enter the Church, she could not reconcile herself to the fundamental tenets of either the Catholic or
Anglican Church, writing: "The Incarnation—the Trinity—the
Atonement seem to be abortions of a comprehension of God's
plan."[9] Her concept of a lawful, benevolent God precluded any belief in miracles (as interruptions of God's laws) or eternal damnation, and thus she read the Scriptures critically and figuratively
rather than literally.

A year later she traveled to Ireland to visit hospitals in Dublin
and Belfast, and in 1853 she traveled to Paris where she resided
with the Sisters of Charity, working in their orphanage and hospital and inspecting other facilities in the city. Upon her return to
England, she accepted a position in as superintendent of a women's
hospital in London. The necessary separation from her family was
now complete. Barely a year passed when, at the invitation of Sidney Herbert, the Secretary at War, she led a team of thirty-eight
nurses to the war-torn Crimea and a legend was born. She was
henceforth to have the purposeful life she had dreamed of since
her adolescence.

Yet despite the many years of service to come, a sense of despair, hopelessness, and resignation continued to plague her to the
end of her days. This is particularly true following the deaths of
her closest associates, most notably Sidney Herbert and Arthur
Hugh Clough in 1861. Her Bible is extensively marked in the 1860s
and 1870s, revealing the depths of her depression. Among the passages marked in Job was chapter 17, verse 11: "My days have passed,
my plans are shattered, and so are the desires of my heart." At
Psalm 18, which begins "The cords of death entangeled me", she

---

8. Shane Leslie, "Forgotten Passages in the Life of Florence Nightingale," *The Dublin Review*, vol. 161, no. 323 (October 1917): p. 185.

9. *Suggestions for Thought* (Calabria & Macrae), p. 13.

wrote "This world *is* hell." She repeatedly turned to Psalm 69: "Save me, O God, for the waters have come up to my neck, I sink in the miry depths . . ."; to Lamentations 3: "I am the man who has seen affliction by the rod of his wrath . . ."; and to a passage in Acts of the Apostles, in which Jesus speaks of Saul (9:16): "I will show him how much he must suffer for my name."

At the same time, she also turned to Thomas à Kempis's medieval classic *The Imitation of Christ*. Here too, she copiously marked passages reflecting her pain and despair, consistently underlining those passages that speak of the necessity of suffering for spiritual advancement: "God desires that you learn to bear trials without comfort. . . . If you bear the cross willingly, it will bear you. . . . The further a man advances in the spiritual life, the heavier and more numerous he finds the crosses" (Book 2, chapter 12). In Book I, Chapter 22, she underlined: "Truly it is a misery to live upon the earth"; and in chapter 23, she marked "Each morning remember that you may not live until evening," adding in her own hand: "Oh how glad I should be."

Feminist interpretations continue to point to "Cassandra" to substantiate the view that Nightingale's psychological problems arose from a lack of personal fulfillment as a woman. This is true in part, but consider that "Cassandra," comprises only thirty-seven of *Suggestions for Thought*'s 829 pages, the bulk of the work being devoted to theological and philosophical questions. Thus, the question remains, if Nightingale's alleged "hysteria" resulted solely from the lack of meaningful activity, how do we explain the depression she suffered in the years after the Crimean War that were filled with research and writing *Notes on Matters Affecting the Health, Efficiency and Hospital Administration of the British Army* (1858), *Notes on Hospitals* (1858), *Notes on Nursing* (1859), *Suggestions for Thought* (1860), *Notes on Lying-in Institutions* (1871), as well as countless reports, papers, and pamphlets? The best explanation is perhaps to be found within the framework of the mystical model: having experienced the transcendent reality of God on several occasions, Nightingale was nevertheless unable to make that final leap to the unitive life whereby the individual ceases to perceive themselves as separate and apart from God, becoming one with God—a subject addressed repeatedly in *Suggestions for Thought*, her most extensive writing. Still, we must ask why she was unable to make this final step given her profound sense of spirituality? Although transcendence is ultimately a mystery, I believe the answer may be attributed in part to the fact that much of Nightingale's work to reform military health care thrust her into harsh political and personal battles that angered and frustrated her endlessly. She could despise her adversaries as intensely as she could love devoted friends and family. Unable to extricate herself from worldy squabbles and her own personal disappointments and failures, she would continue to vacillate between episodes of joy and hopelessness for many years to come, never to know the ecstasy of complete transcendent unity with the Divine.

The nineteenth century produced many women who undertook social reform in the name of God—women such as Elizabeth Fry, who sought to reform Britain's prison system, Josephine Butler, advocate of women's rights and opponent of the Contagious Diseases Act; and Octavia Hill, who established housing for the poor. What sets Florence Nightingale apart from many of her contemporaries is the great spiritual crisis she endured to discern God's will. In this respect she is most like the American reformer Dorothea Dix, who took up the plight of the mentally insane in the United States and abroad. Although Dix had an unstable childhood as the daughter of an alcoholic, Methodist lay-preacher, like Nightingale she too believed that God called her to service, and she suffered great mental and physical anguish until she discovered her divinely appointed mission. Upon awakening to God's will, both women sacrificed the opportunity to marry. As Nightingale developed her theories of nursing by observing hospital care in Britain, and Europe, so did Dix visit jails and asylums over much of the eastern United States, Britain and Europe, recording her obervations. Both women became interested in a variety of social issues, including education for the deaf and dumb as well as prison reform. Coincidentally both became associates of Samuel Gridley Howe, the American educator and legislator, and the Rathbones, a family of British philanthropists and reformers. Like Nightingale, Dix became a formidable force in the political arena, commanding the respect of congressmen and presidents alike. Inspired by reports of Nightingale's work in the Crimea, Dix twice attempted to meet her: once at Scutari, but Nightingale had taken ill at the hospital at Balaclava, and once after Nightingale had returned to England but was still too ill to receive visitors. When the American Civil War broke out, Dix seized the opportunity to emulate Nightingale and was appointed Superintendent of Women Nurses for the Union. "I think my duty lies near the military Hospitals for the present," she wrote. The similarities between Dix and Nightingale were soon seen: an engraving from *Godey's Lady's Book* of 1861 depicts both Dix and Nightingale as the ideal of female heroism.[10] Millard Fillmore told Dix: "In all that adorns the female character, she [Nightingale] has no parallel but yourself," and Louisa May Alcott referred to Dix as "our Florence Nightingale." (Unfortunately, Dix emulated Nightingale to a fault and became known for her stubborness and inability to compromise and take orders from superiors.)[11]

In *The Way of Perfection*, St. Teresa of Avila's classic guide to prayer, she admonished her sisters that an ardent desire to be with God can cause someone to lose her reason:

> I saw this happen to someone not long ago; she was of an impetuous nature, but so accustomed to curbing her will that, from what I had seen at other times, I thought her will was completely annihilated; yet, when I saw her for a moment, the great stress and strain caused by her efforts to hide her feelings had all but destroyed her reason.[12]

The passage is, of course, generally considered to be autobiographical, yet, as the earlier-going diary and discussion demonstrates, it could just as well be applied to Nightingale. Confused and frustrated by a divine call that upset the tranquility of her upper-class family life, Nightingale gleaned ancient Egyptian, Platonic, and Hermetic philosophy; Christian scripture; and the works of poets, mystics, and missionaries in an attempt to understand the nature of God

10. Patricia Okker, *Our Sister Editors: Sarah J. Hale and the Tradition of Nineteenth-Century American Women Editors* (Athens, Ga.: University of Georgia Press, 1995, p. 117.) My thanks to Douglas Duchin, Newman Library, Baruch College, for bringing this engraving to my attention.

11. David Gollaher, *Voice for the Mad: the Life of Dorothea Dix* (New York: The Free Press, 1995).

12. *The Way of Perfection*; translated and edited by E. Allison Peers (New York: Doubleday, 1964), pp. 143 (ch. 19).

and her role in the divine plan. On her trip to Egypt and Greece she journeyed back into antiquity, identifying with some of the greatest individuals in the history of religion and philosophy: separated from her mother and set adrift on the Nile, she was as Moses on a quest to find God and bring her people to a new and better understanding of Him; she was as Plato, returning to Greece after uncovering the wisdom of the Egyptians. She was as Christ agonizing on the Mount of Olives praying to have the cup taken from her, as Paul preaching in Athens, and finally she was the virgin consecrated to the service of God, 'the handmaiden of the Lord.'

Ever since Lytton Strachey's *Eminent Victorians* (1918), some writers have sought to emphasize Nightingale's character weaknesses, pointing to her manic depression, hypochondria, ruthlessness in personal relations, and ambition to prove that the idol of the British soldier had clay feet. Using Nightingale's own remarks about sacrificing her reputuation (March 7, 8, and 10) as ammunition, F. B. Smith delivered the most vociferous assault, arguing that a concern for reputation and power was *the* driving force behind her life's work. While there is no doubt that Nightingale wanted to make some impact on the world and would later wield tremendous influence among military and government officials as she proceeded with her health reforms, perhaps even relishing such authority, consider the woman who, after being hailed a national heroine in the Crimea, returned to England incognito, arriving back at her home unannounced, and thereafter shunned all public attention. Consider the woman who formed Parliamentary committees, wrote their reports with no acknowledgment, and privately recorded: "I only wish to be forgotten." [13] Finally, consider if Nightingale had been a man, would she have been criticized for being overzealous and ambitious?

Furthermore, it must be admitted that the aforegoing diary and 'visions' clearly indicate that Nightingale exhibited many traits in common with some of the greatest mystic saints of Christendom: she heard God call her into service, sought only to do what she believed to be God's will while enduring fierce opposition from her family, and longed to serve humanity and alleviate suffering. Indeed, in recent years the Episcopal Church in the United States

---

13. She wrote this in her copy of *The Imitation of Christ* (Book I, ch. 23) now in the Florence Nightingale Museum.

even considered adding her name to their calendar of saints as did the Church of England, and as the Canadian Church had already done.[14] An individual who has had an impact on the world to the extent Nightingale did cannot, however, be easily classified as neurotic, saint, or otherwise. It has not been my purpose here to canonize this remarkable woman, but rather to reveal a part of her that few, if any, ever saw or ever knew. At the end of "Cassandra," in a moment of clarity unclouded by bitterness or resentment, depression or despair, Nightingale provided us with her own epitaph:

> Let neither name nor date be placed on her grave, still less the expression of regret or of admiration; but simply the words, 'I believe in God.'

---

14. Larry Witham, "Episcopalians Ponder Sundry List of Saints," *Washington Times*, July 19, 1991, p. F5; Geoffrey Wheatcroft, "Saint George Orwell Would Be Better," *Independent*, July 16, 1995, p. 25.

Bibliography

Allchin, A. M. *The Silent Rebellion: Anglican Religious Communities, 1845–1900.* London: SCM, 1958.

Allen, Donald R. "Florence Nightingale: Toward a Psychohistorical Interpretation," *Journal of Interdisciplinary History,* 6:1 (Summer 1975), pp. 23–45.

Angela of Foligno: Complete Works (Paul Lachance, trans.) New York: Paulist Press, 1993.

Bell, H. Idris. *Cults and Creeds in Graeco-Roman Egypt.* Chicago: Ares, 1985 reprint.

Bishop, W. J., and Sue Goldie. *A Bio-Bibliography of Florence Nightingale.* London: Dawsons of Pall Mall, 1962.

Boyd, Nancy. *Three Victorian Women Who Changed Their World: Josephine Butler, Octavia Hill, Florence Nightingale.* New York: Oxford University Press, 1982.

Brontë, Charlotte. *Shirley.* London: Penguin, 1985.

Bullough, Verne, and Bonnie Bullough. *The Care of the Sick: the Emergence of Modern Nursing.* New York: Prodist, 1978.

Bunsen, Frances Baroness. *Memoirs of Baron Bunsen.* 2nd ed. Philadelphia: J. B. Lippincott, 1869.

Calabria, Michael D. "Spiritual Insights of Florence Nightingale," *The Quest,* vol. 3, no. 2 (Summer 1990): 66–74.

Catherine of Genoa. *Purgation & Purgatory, The Spiritual Dialogue.* New York: Paulist Press, 1979.

Cook, Sir Edward. *The Life of Florence Nightingale.* 2 vols. London: Macmillan, 1913.

Daschke, Dereck M. "Individuation and the Psychology of the Mystic Union," *Journal of Psychology and Christianity,* vol. 12, no. 3 (1993): 245–52.

Faderman, Lillian. *Surpassing the Love of Men: Romantic Friendship and Love Between Women from the Renaissance to the Present.* New York: William Morrow, 1981.

Frawley, Maria H. "Desert Places/Gendered Spaces: Victorian Women in the Middle East," *Nineteenth Century Contexts,* vol. 15, no. 1 (1991): 49–64.

Gertrud the Great of Helfta, *Spiritual Exercises*. (Gertrud Jaron Lewis and Jack Lewis, trans.) Kalamazoo, Mich.: Cistercian Publications, 1989.

Gollaher, David. *Voice for the Mad: the Life of Dorothea Dix*. New York: The Free Press, 1995.

Gordon, Lyndall. *Charlotte Bronte: a Passionate Life*. London: Vintage, 1995.

Head, Joseph, and S. L. Cranston, comps. *Reincarnation: an East-West Anthology*. Wheaton, Ill.: Theosophical Publishing House, 1968.

Hoecker-Drysdale, Susan. *Harriet Martineau: First Woman Sociologist*. Oxford: Berg, 1992.

Iversen, Erik. *Egyptian and Hermetic Doctrine*. Copenhagen: Museum Tusculanum Press, 1984.

James, William. *The Varieties of Religious Experience*. New York: Collier, 1961.

Jenkins, Ruth Y. *Reclaiming Myths of Power: Women Writers and the Victorian Spiritual Crisis*. Lewisberg, Pa.: Bucknell University Press, 1995.

John of the Cross. *Selected Writings*. New York: Paulist Press, 1987.

Keele, Mary, ed. *Florence Nightingale in Rome: Letters Written by Florence Nightingale in Rome in the Winter of 1847–1848*. Memoirs of the American Philosophical Society, no. 143. Philadelphia: American Philosophical Society, 1981.

King, James. *William Cowper: a Biography*. Durham, N.C.: Duke University Press, 1986.

Leslie, Shane. "Forgotten Passages in the Life of Florence Nightingale," *The Dublin Review*, vol. 161, no. 323 (October 1917): 179–98.

Life of Amelia Wilhemina Sieveking. Catherine Winkworth, ed. London: Longman et al., 1863.

Life of Pastor Fliedner of Kaiserswerth, Catherine Winkworth, trans., (London: Longmans, Green, 1867).

Martineau, Harriet. *Eastern Life: Past and Present*. 3 vols. London: Edward Moxon, 1848.

Martyn, Henry. *Memoir of the Rev. Henry Martyn*. New York: Protestant Episcopal Society for the Promotion of Evangelical Knowledge, 1858.

Nightingale, Florence. *Letters from Egypt.* London: A. & G. A. Spottiswoode, 1854.

———. *Letters from Egypt: a Journey on the Nile, 1849–1850.* New York: Weidenfeld & Nicolson, 1987.

———. *Cassandra and Other Selections from Suggestions for Thought.* Edited by Mary Poovey. NYU Press Women's Classics. New York: New York University Press, 1992.

———. *Suggestions for Thought: Selections and Commentaries.* Edited by Michael D. Calabria and Janet A. Macrae. Philadelphia: University of Pennsylvania Press, 1994.

O'Malley, I. B. *Florence Nightingale: 1820–1856: a Study of Her Life Down to the End of the Crimean War.* London: Thorton Butterworth, 1931.

Pichanick, Valerie Kossew. *Harriet Martineau: the Woman and Her Work, 1802–76.* Ann Arbor: University of Michigan Press, 1980.

Podvoll, Edward Mitchell. "Psychosis and the Mystic Path," *The Psychoanalytic Review,* vol. 66, no. 4 (1979): 571–90.

Pope-Hennessy, James. *Monckton Milnes.* 2 vols. London: Constable, 1949–51.

Prelinger, Catherine M. "The Nineteeth-Century Deaconessate in Germany: the Efficacy of a Family Model," in *German Women in the Eighteenth and Nineteenth Centuries: a Social and Literary History.* Ruth-Ellen B. Joeres and Mary Jo Maynes, eds. Bloomington: Indiana University Press, 1985, pp. 215–29.

Rees, Joan. *Writings on the Nile: Harriet Martineau, Florence Nightingale, Amelia Edwards.* London: Rubicon, 1995.

Richards, Dell. *Superstars: Twelve Lesbians Who Changed the World.* New York: Carroll & Graf, 1993.

Sattin, Anthony. *Lifting the Veil: British Society in Egypt, 1768–1956.* London: J. M. Dent & Sons, 1988.

Scott, Walter (ed.). *Hermetica.* S.l., Solos Press, n.d.

Shaddock, Jennifer. "Florence Nightingale's Notes on Nursing as Survival Memoir," *Literature and Medicine,* vol. 14, no. 1 (Spring 1995): 23–35.

Shiman, Lilian Lewis. *Women and Leadership in Nineteenth-Century England.* New York: St. Martin's Press, 1992.

Showalter, Elaine. "Florence Nightingale's Feminist Complaint: Women, Religion, and *Suggestions for Thought*," *Journal of Women in Culture and Society,* vol. 6, no. 3 (1981): 395–412.

———. *The Female Malady: Women, Madness, and English Culture, 1830–1980.* New York: Penguin, 1985.

Smith, F. B. *Florence Nightingale: Reputation and Power.* New York: St. Martin's Press, 1982.

Stephen, John Lloyd. *Incidents of Travel in Egypt, Arabia Petraea, and the Holy Land,* Victor Wolfgang von Hagen, ed. San Francisco: Chronicle Books, 1991.

Sticker, Anna. *Florence Nightingale: Curriculum Vitae.* Dusseldorf–Kaiserswerth: Diakoniwerk, 1965.

Strachey, Ray. *The Cause: A Short History of the Women's Movement in Great Britain.* London: G. Bell, 1928.

Teresa of Avila, Saint. *The Way of Perfection.* E. Allison Peters, trans. New York: Doubleday, 1964.

———. *The Interior Castle.* Kieran Kavanaugh and Otilio Rodriguez, trans. New York: Paulist Press, 1979.

———. *The Collected Works.* Vol. 1: The Book of Her Life, Spiritual Testimonies, Soliloquies. 2nd rev. ed. Kieran Kavanaugh and Otilio Rodriguez, trans. Washington, D.C.: Institute of Carmelite Studies, 1987.

Thomas, Gillian. *Harriet Martineau.* Boston: Twayne, 1985.

Underhill, Evelyn. *Mysticism: A Study in the Nature and Development of Man's Spiritual Consciousness.* New York: New American Library, 1974.

Vicinus, Martha, and Bea Nergaard, eds. *Ever Yours, Florence Nightingale: Selected Letters.* Cambridge, Mass.: Harvard University Press, 1990.

Widerquist, JoAnn G. "Florence Nightingale's Calling," *Second Opinion,* vol. 17, no. 3 (January 1992): 108–21.

———. "The Spirituality of Florence Nightingale," *Nursing Research,* vol. 41, no. 1 (January/February 1992): 49–55.

Woodham-Smith, Cecil. *Florence Nightingale: 1829–1910.* New York: McGraw-Hill, 1951.

Yates, Frances A. *Giordano Bruno and the Hermetic Tradition.* Chicago: University of Chicago Press, 1991.

Subject Index

Index of Place Names

EGYPT

A

Aboo Simbel (var. Ipsamboul; mod. Abu Simbel), 18, 23–25, 91–92
Abydos, 45
Alexandria, 18, 51, 53
Apolloinopolis Magna, 34
Armant (Hermonthis), 20
Asaseef, 40–41
Asouan (Aswan), 21, 34

B

Beit el Wellee (Beit el-Wali), 26, 27n
Bidji, 32
Birket Habu, 41

C

Cairo, 18, 47, 50–51

D

Dakka, 25n, 93
Dabod, 30
Dayr el Bahree (Deir el-Bahri), 40, 121, 123, 124–25
Dayr el Medeeneh (Deir el-Medineh), 40
Dendera, 43
Derr, 22, 23n

E

Edfoo (Edfu), 34
Eilethyia (El-Kab), 35n
Ekhmim (Panopolis), 45
Elephantine, 21, 34
Esne (Esna), 21, 35–36

F

Fostat (Fustat), 47

G

Gebel Shekh Heredee, 45
Gerf Hossein, 26
Girgeh, 45

H

Hagar Silsilis (Hadjar Silsileh, Gebel el-Silsila), 21, 34
Heliopolis, 48
How (Diosopolis Parva), 43

I

Ibreem (Qasr Ibrim), 25

J

Jerf Hossayn (Gerf Hossein), 25

GREECE, ITALY, ETC.